Anaïs Nin:
An Unprofessional Study

Praise for *Anaïs Nin: An Unprofessional Study*:

In *Anaïs Nin: An Unprofessional Study*, Kazim Ali has written a remarkable work of poetic scholarship that will appeal as much to those who started reading Nin's diaries, fiction, and essays decades ago as it will to relative newcomers to her oeuvre. As one of the "old-timers" myself, I found that reading Ali's study transported me back to Nin's fictional world and recreated, as well, a sense of what it was like to discover that world as a young scholar. Ali also provides fresh ways of understanding Nin's artistic process. For example, among Ali's insights is how Nin's fiction might have provided a structure within which she shaped *The Diary of Anaïs Nin, Volumes I-VI*, for publication. Unconventional as it is insightful, *Anaïs Nin: An Unprofessional Study* also provides an artist's perspective on Nin's fictional characters, especially on the fluidity among them. What some critics saw as a lack of realism in Nin's fiction, Ali presents as an evolution of psychic development over the various renditions of the stories. Perhaps most innovative within these pages are Ali's stage set designs, dance performance proposals, and museum installation blueprints, which anchor Nin's themes in a compelling visual and auditory imaginary. In keeping with Nin's sense that what is imagined and internal is as real—or more real—than what is "factual" and external, Ali captures the magic that Nin embraced—that of one's life as a work of art.

—Diane Richard-Allerdyce, Ph.D., author
of *Anaïs Nin and the Remaking of Self:
Gender, Modernism, and Narrative Recovery*

Ali's analysis of Anaïs Nin's fiction is a welcome addition to Nin scholarship. His pleasure in her writing is apparent in each passage, written with his precise and poetic language that keeps the text imaginative and energetic. *Anaïs Nin: An Unprofessional Study* is a meditation on her fiction, following Nin's own *DH Lawrence: An Unprofessional Study*, showing a similar reverence for an admired writer. Ali uncovers, demystifies, and unites images, characters, and even small parts of Nin's biography. This is the book we've been waiting for, to have a passionate wordsmith deeply delve into the fiction and guide us through it.

—Steven Reigns, Anaïs Nin scholar & Inaugural Poet Laureate of West Hollywood, CA

Also by Kazim Ali:

Poetry:

The Far Mosque
The Fortieth Day
Sky Ward
All One's Blue

Fiction:

Quinn's Passage
The Disappearance of Seth
Uncle Sharif's Life in Music
The Secret Room: A String Quartet

Essays/Nonfiction:

Orange Alert: Essays on Poetry, Art, and
the Architecture of Silence
Resident Alien: On Border-Crossing and
the Undocumented Divine
Fasting for Ramadan: Notes from a Spiritual Practice

Cross-Genre:

Bright Felon: Autobiography and Cities
Wind Instrument

Anaïs Nin:
An Unprofessional Study

Kazim Ali

Agape Editions
Los Angeles, CA

Published by Agape Editions
http://agapeeditions.com
Los Angeles, CA

Copyright © 2017 by Kazim Ali
All rights reserved

Cover image: *Anaïs Before the Glass*, by Andy Nava.
Graphite on paper. 2016.
Used by kind permission of the artist.

Cover & interior design: Lauren A. Pirosko

Editor: Fox Frazier-Foley
Associate Editor: Jasmine An
Assistant Editors: Jane Huffman, Jacqueline Vega, and Lauren Perlaki

Agape Editions titles are printed using Lightning Source
and distributed by Ingram Content Group.

This title is also for purchase directly from the publisher.

Library of Congress
Cataloguing-in-Publication Data
Anaïs Nin: An Unprofessional Study // Kazim Ali
Library of Congress Control Number 2016935283
Ali, Kazim
ISBN 978-1-939675-37-8

9 8 7 6 5 4 3 2 1

FIRST EDITION

Contents

Preface	...4
Overture	...10
Houses	...18
Dance	...32
A Design for a Choreography: *Children of Albatross*	...46
Music	...54
A Symphony (with Notes by Anaïs Nin)	...68
Film	...74
A Spy in the House of Love: A Film Treatment	...86
Painting	...98
Instruction Painting: A Blueprint for an Installation	...112
Boats	...120
The Voice	...132
Coda	...144
Bibliography	...155
Acknowledgments	...159
About the Author	...161

Preface

I came to Anaïs Nin first as a reader, not as a student and not as a lover, and definitely not as a scholar. Desperate for poetry in prose, hungry for a fiction that moved musically and intuitively and not according to some preordained idea of story or plot—in other words, a fiction that truly represented LIFE as it is lived and was not a mere archeology or anthropology or rehearsal of old tropes—I combed through the library shelves and found one day a book called *Children of the Albatross*. It changed my idea of what literature could do, and just when I thought I might understand I found *House of Incest*. Then *Winter of Artifice*. It wasn't until after I had learned her fiction that I found Nin's *Diary,* first through *Henry and June,* and then through all the incarnations that preceded and followed.

Nin was my first professor of literature and she guided me when every other beacon felt forced, felt unreal, felt untrue. For twenty years, I followed her in the dark, writing this book in my head, with my body on stages and in beds, in music in the air.

Finally, one late summer, as the young Nin did with her book on Lawrence, I wrote quickly, impressionistically and (mainly) from memory.

Nin has been understood in three stages—the first in which only her fiction was known, then once the *Diary* began appearing a more complete assessment was possible, and then finally once Hugh Guiler passed away portions of the so-called "unexpurgated" *Diary* were released bit by slow bit.

It is tempting to say that what still remains is for another scholar to go now to the original diary manuscripts, to put together "expurgated" and "unexpurgated" and find the whole view. The diary of the last years of Nin's life, wracked by illness, have by her own design been so far withheld. When will we, her readers, have access to an "unedited" Nin? Though Nin herself warned that sometimes there is no heart of the matter but only the continually unfolding veils of meaning. She viewed her *Diary* as a work of literature in and of itself, and revised and edited it as such. Sometimes this revision practice resulted in destroying originals.

Nin exists, will always exist perhaps, as she does now: in waves of revelation, one after the other, each changing the ones before it but reflecting forward onto what might come next.

The earlier generation of critics, who did not have access to the "unexpurgated" diaries published since the death of Nin's husband Hugh Guiler, mainly treated the *Diary* separately from the novel, and the new generation of critics chose either to view the Diary as a genesis for the fiction (if they privileged the fiction) or the fiction as a way of publishing material Nin felt she couldn't publish as nonfiction. Most all of the critics who have written on Nin favor a work-by-work approach, with the exceptions of Sharon Spencer and Evelyn Hinz who mostly treated the works holistically and looked for common themes. Later critics have had access to the full range of diaries as well as to extensive biographies by Noel Riley Fitch and Deirdre Bair, and so their approaches have necessarily shifted to include the study of autobiographical influences, the relationship between fiction and nonfiction, and Nin's revision practices.

I do something different in this book, which is to (mostly) leave aside the biographical and the autobiographical and go back to the novels, the novellas, the short stories, the prose poem-like early writings and consider Nin as a fiction writer, an artisan, an artist. Rather than do the proper thing, which might be to engage in a more systematic exploration of her themes and theories, I am a dilettante here, a guest at a party who moves from one conversation to another. Chapters on Nin's localities—houses and boats and at least twice actual houseboats—frame more lyrical explorations of the relation of Nin's writing with painting, music and dance.

At any rate, I am first and foremost a poet, and all the architecture of my own prose work, whether novel or essay or something in between, is the architecture of poetry. This book is no different.

My models in the approach of this book were not the scholars whose work I nonetheless very much appreciate and honor and admire—Bettina Knapp, Oliver Evans, Sharon Spencer, Evelyn Hinz, Diane Allerdyce-Richard, Helen Tookey, Philip K. Jason, Anne Salvatore, and Suzanne Nalbantian, to name only a few who have written beautiful and illuminating books about Nin—but rather Anaïs Nin herself, in her work on D.H. Lawrence, Hoshang Merchant's book on Nin, and others: Susan Howe's book on Emily Dickinson, Charles Olson's rapture on Herman Melville, and very particularly Stephen Collis' book on Susan Howe where he really makes the case for the 'amateur critic.'

So perhaps I misspoke. It *is* as a student I engaged these

texts—wanting always to know more, know deeper. It is even as a scholar that I sought to understand Nin's intentions and influences. And yes, it is as a lover that I engage with these texts—exploratory, messy, confused, clumsy, but always hungry, and most earnestly, always wanting to elicit from the writing itself a concordant corresponding groan of pleasure at my ministrations.

To touch as I had been touched. In every place.

—K.A.
Toronto, 7/2016

Overture

Reading a novel by Anaïs Nin can feel like watching motion on the other side of a veil or listening to music being played in the next room.

My favorite story about Emily Dickinson is the one where she stops on the other side of the door to listen to the music.

I thought: maybe it is not that she is afraid to go in and look at the musicians directly, but this is a purer way of listening.

Our disconnections from reality, our hang-ups due to past experiences or misunderstanding and misapprehension, those things that stop us from experiencing life fully and openly are part of our deepest and innermost core, according to classical Vedantic philosophy.

Events slide by in a Nin novel because maybe events do slide by.

You see them as if through a veil because in life you live always struggling to be more real, see past occlusion, more present to your own experiences.

Nin moves between "eros"—the physical and therefore ultimately unKNOWable— and "psyche," the mental, the searcher, the one that always WANTS to know but never can.

In the myth Psyche, of course, was not permitted to look directly. She could have Eros, but only if she made love to him in the dark. Eros knew: true knowledge can be had in the dark—it is by direct bodily experience of touch, smell, taste.

From an old house in Louveciennes, on the outskirts of Paris, Anaïs Nin, self-described "banker's wife," felt herself wake up and cast off the bonds of conventionality in sexuality, in fiction, and ultimately in the two places sexuality and fiction both met— her own body, and in the diary she wrote throughout her life.
The house in Louveciennes is the starting point of her diary— which I have already explained is not just one "Diary" but a series of different incarnations that flower out one from the other. It appears again in *The House of Incest,* neither poetry nor prose, neither essay nor novel; or perhaps all of these things.

Again in *Children of the Albatross,* the same house appears, this time as the home of Djuna.

For Nin, a model turned banker's wife, a life as a dancer in Paris brought her back to herself as an artist. Later still, the movements of the dance themselves served as a model for the structure of a novel.

As the novel's parts unbuckled themselves from conventional notions of plot, so too did her residence. At first traveling between Louveciennes and Henry Miller's flat in Clichy, she eventually found her own space:

Floating between worlds, between genres, Nin chose a houseboat on the river.

An old decrepit houseboat turned into a garden shed is the *mise-en-scène* for the first story in *The Waste of Timelessness*. The boat sails down the river and disappears in the story "Houseboat" from *Under a Glass Bell*.

A full life is lived in the houseboat in *Four-Chambered Heart*.

The refractions of sense and location are told through the repeating image of Duchamp's painting *Nude Descending a Staircase,* which appears in several different Nin novels in a passage repeated word for word. In *Spy in the House of Love,* the description of the woman in the painting refers to Sabina; in *Four-Chambered Heart* the same passage refers to Djuna. Critic Oliver Evans finds this a major weakness in Nin's treatment of character, causing Sabina and Djuna to "blur and overlap in the reader's mind."[1]

Nin is saying something more revolutionary about character here: that these two women, clearly opposed to each other, could share an aspect, just like the fractured woman in the Duchamp painting.

Could be the same woman. Or could be different women. Djuna. Sabina.

To Djuna is given the house of Nin in *Children of the Albatross*.

To a different Djuna, in a book Nin called *The Winter of Artifice*, published once and then never re-printed, and then to Lillian in *Ladders to Fire* and then to Jay in *Spy in the House of Love*, is given the description of Nin's first meeting with June Miller. In *The House of Incest* it is the nameless narrator who sees June Miller's face walking toward her from the dark garden. Characters blur and overlap in the reader's mind.

---

1. Oliver Evans, *Anaïs Nin* (Carbondale: Southern Illinois University Press, 1968), 160.

Events and characters unfold like figures seen in a film. Time moves spatially rather than chronologically. Novels as street performance. Or as Kazuko Sagisaki wrote, as Noh Play.

The collages of Jean Varda: described again and again in her late novel *Collages*. Novel as a collage or a painting rescued from a burning house.

Children of the Albatross written with sudden entrances and exits to simulate the energy of youth. Novel as ballet.

A novel made up of parts that play one against the other. Seen then as a sculpture in space, to be seen from various sides and aspects. This is worked through in the micro-structure of the individual novel *Spy in the House of Love,* and on a macro-level in *Cities of the Interior,* Nin's "continuous novel," called by Sharon Spencer a "mobile in space," and then realized again in a structure combining both of these forms in her final novel *Collages.*

You can't read the novels for solely the narrative, though a story is there, but must experience them lyrically. A thousand clarifications, expansions, developments, stream off of the individual books into later books, books that develop and change as the years go by, the diaries that slowly appear and accrete new versions of each revealing new truths and sources—

And other books, disappeared books: *The Winter of Artifice. Stella. This Hunger. Solar Barque.* Not disappeared. Dissipated among other books (one chapter of *The Winter of Artifice* evaporates, the first chapter of *This Hunger,* called "Stella," takes its place). Books are reformed. Stories travel and are absorbed. Adsorbed. Resorbed.

If Nin is Salome dancing with seven veils, it is not really important to know the "truth" of anything but to see the actual dance, the movement of the veil.

It helps you yourself learn how to read and know yourself. Psyche gave herself voice by raising the lantern to finally look.

This book, which whose title does not have a "the" in it, is a markedly different book than its similarly named predecessor.

Stella, first from *This Hunger* but then from *Winter of Artifice,* looks at herself on the screen wondering what is really real there.

But, unlike what I always believed, the myth of Psyche doesn't end with her forbidden glimpse of the nude Eros, his vanishing. In order to regain her love, taken from her as punishment for her transgression, like Hercules, Psyche undertakes several labors. In order to prove herself worthy.

Nin created a tradition and space for work that transcends lines between lyric and narrative, between prose and poetry. Contemporary writers working in a form called the "lyric novel," writers like Carole Maso and Fanny Howe, have been able to fuse both Eros and Psyche in novels in the shapes of both houses and boats that Nin helped to design and inhabit.

At the end of my novel *Quinn's Passage,* Quinn floats in the ocean, wondering what's next.

Sharon Spencer writes, "Her style and her structure are intimately related to the nonverbal arts of painting, dance and music, not only in the obvious sense that she writes about artists, but more deeply, because she has so brilliantly adapted techniques of other arts to prose."[2]

In *Novel of the Future,* Nin writes, "I have chosen to write about artists...because the artist usually lives with a greater

---

2. Anaïs Nin, *Cities of the Interior*, with an introduction by Sharon Spencer, (Athens: Ohio University Press, 1980), xvii.

spontaneity than the nonartists."³ What she was really interested in were characters who were invested in the process of self-discovery while living their lives.

In the end, what Nin really wants is to give you the ability to look always closer.

---

3. Nin, *The Novel of the Future* (Athens: Ohio University Press, 1968), 21.

Houses

At the very start, Nin made her house in Louveciennes a mythic one, the one with the extra shutter and secret room. Perhaps she needed to mythologize a place after a life of wandering. Certainly the structure of "place" would become a defining characteristic of both Nin's fiction and life.

Later on, after she came to New York, there was Nin's apartment in Washington Square Village, haven for artistic and wayward youth of all kinds.

To this apartment came all of Nin's young comrades—Paul, Bill, Pablo, Leonard, Lawrence—depicted later in *Diary IV,* the so-called "Children of the Albatross."

And after that, the House of Light, called so by its designer Eric Lloyd Wright, who designed it for Nin and his stepson, Nin's second husband, Rupert Pole.

The wide open house had only three rooms in it, looking out over the pool, without chairs, only low cushions and tables in the Japanese style.

And, conceptually, other "houses": the birdcage of her

own neuroses that she wore around her head to Kenneth Anger's "Come as Your Madness" party, and later, in the film *Inauguration of the Pleasure Dome*. The basket in which she carried around her diary as a young girl. The diary itself. The mythic houses that appear in her books.

But where Nin became a woman, where she staged her own rebirth, as a writer, as a woman, as a student of psychoanalysis, was the house at Louveciennes, the house she and Hugo came to live in when they moved out of Paris in 1930.

In this house, where each room was painted a different color to associate with different emotions—"the room of the heart in Chinese lacquer red, the room of the mind in pale green or the brown of philosophy, the room of the body in shell rose, the attic of memory with closets full of the musk of the past"—Nin first met Henry Miller, his wife June, and awakened herself to a life of passion and the life of a writer.[1] It was there that she wrote her first several books, as well as the stories that would many years later be published as *Waste of Timelessness*.

The house is nearly a pilgrimage site: how many of Nin's readers have trekked through the Paris suburbs to find it, to pose by the gate, to perhaps bravely venture inside? Everyone I know who has been there talks of the kindness of the owners, the awareness they have of the transformative energies that must reside there.

Nin writes in her diary of choosing the house because "it had no cellar...one could take root here, feel as one with the house and garden, take nourishment from them like the plants."[2] The passage is later transposed exactly into the novel *Children of the Albatross*.[3]

---

1. Nin, *Cities*, 143.
2. Nin, *The Diary of Anaïs Nin, Volume 1, 1931-34* (n.p.: Harcourt Brace Jovanovich, 1966), 4.
3. Nin, *Cities*, 142.

The line between diary and novel is always so porous crossing one over into the other. Nin admits to an interviewer later that most of the women in *Cities of the Interior* have analogs in the diary. Though are not her, she is careful to say.

Except Lillian, of whom she curiously remarks, "If you read the diaries you'll find the models for all those women but Lillian, whom I took pains to leave as a fictional character."[4]

What an odd way of saying it—"to leave as a fictional character." Grammatically, it only makes sense if Nin thought of the outline of a character first, then fully created them once finding a model for them in her life later, the way a playwright or screenwriter might create a role specifically for an actor or actress to play. It is the same dilemma that faces the great writer Judith Sands—herself based on Djuna Barnes, whom Nin denies naming her own character Djuna after—in the late novel *Collages*. Sands, a recluse, must deal with Dr. Mann, visiting from Israel, who insists he is the embodiment of one of Sands' characters. There is an irony of the scene of a character insisting to an author that she wrote about him in her book because Dr. Mann makes this declaration just before meeting Renate, a character whom Nin very deliberately based on the painter Renate Druks.

When Sands meets Renate, the main character of *Collages*—if such a designation can even be given in a novel which is itself a collage—the book folds back on itself and returns to the beginning, a demonstration of the bystander's cryptic comment to the French consul's wife when she declined to gift her needlepoint on account of its unfinished state: "But my dear lady, according to the Koran nothing is ever finished."[5]

As Nin admitted candidly in her last *Diary VII*: "We are all

---

4. Wendy DuBow, ed., *Conversations with Anaïs Nin* (Jackson: University Press of Mississippi, 1994), 127.
5. Nin, *Collages* (Swallow Press, 1964), 91.

fictions. I am a fiction."[6]

There's nothing to explain writings that wonder the hard thought of physical lust and spiritual need—as in her chapter "Bread and Wafer" included in the novel *Ladders to Fire*—the day divided in half, the body moving, seen through glass. One must instead experience them as art.

There's nothing to smooth out a book like this, no discursive description. No characters going to the icebox for a drink or to make a sandwich—"Even in the bathroom there were no medicine bottles on the shelves proclaiming: soda, castor oil, cold cream. She had transferred all of them to alchemist bottles, and the homeliest drug assumed an air of philter."[7]

Instead, the house is a mythical place where encounters of a psychic nature occur.

Nin writes of the twelve windows in the façade of the house: "One shutter was put there for symmetry only, but I often dream about this mysterious room which does not exist behind the closed shutter."[8] When the same house is described in *House of Incest*, the twelve rooms correspond to the twelve signs of the zodiac.

By the time the house reappears as Djuna's house in *Children of the Albatross*, the sealed room is real: "One shutter was closed and corresponded to no room. During some transformation of the house it had been walled up...someday she would discover an entrance to it."[9]

The idea helps us to see the image and the image helps us to see.

---

6. Nin, *The Diary of Anaïs Nin, Volume VII, 1966-1974* (n.p.: Harcourt Brace Jovanovich), 37.
7. Nin, *Cities*, 145-146.
8. Nin, *Diary, Vol. 1*, 4.
9. Nin, *Cities*, 142.

But contrast Djuna's carefully constructed house to Lillian's equally carefully constructed house: "Lillian's house was beautiful, lacquered, grown among the trees"—all traits that seem to compare it favorably with Djuna's house—"but it did not seem to belong to her...it did not have her face, her atmosphere. She always looked like a stranger in it." And of course, Lillian knows why: "Who made the marriage? Who desired the children?...It was as if it happened in her sleep."[10]

In this sense, one imagines Djuna creating the house she herself *needs* rather than inhabiting a physical space defined and given life by others. In *House of Incest,* the strange house with the extra window belongs to Isolina, in later editions called Jeanne. What was for Nin, perhaps, mere architectural oddity, becomes for Jeanne a way of exploring her fraught relationship with her brother, the incest which she cannot face: "In the house of incest there was room which could not be found, a room without a window...where the mind and blood coalesced..." Here both eros and psyche meet within the consciousness of Jeanne.[11]

In order to find her missing brother, Jeanne must find her way to the mysterious room, the one without a window. "Please hang up something out of your windows," she tells the other inhabitants. "Hang up a shawl, or a colored handkerchief, or a rug. I am going out into the garden. I want to see how many windows can be accounted for. I may thus find the room where my brother is hiding from me."[12]

Garden, the source of the elemental earth.

From earth (Louveciennes) to fire (New York) to air (California) to water (the houseboat, the river, the ocean she crosses), Nin

---

10. Ibid, 18.
11. Nin, *House of Incest* (n.p.: Gemor Press, 1947), 40.
12. Ibid, 43.

would traverse and re-traverse these elements in search of fusion, an alchemy.

Symbolically, these four elements meet in the Acapulco of *Diary IV* ("The definition of "tropics" is change and I felt a new woman would be born here."[13]) described as Golconda in the novel *Solar Barque* (later incorporated into *Seduction of the Minotaur*). Lillian chooses the name Golconda for the city because she wants it to be mythical, transformative. It is the first time in any of the novels that one of Nin's heroines chooses and enacts her own catharsis. In all of the previous novels of the cycle, the catharsis is instigated by someone else.

In the garden of Louveciennes, the appearance of fire first gives life to the earth—Anaïs first met June Miller, one of those incidents, like the glimpse young Marguerite Duras caught of Anne-Marie Stretter as her limousine window glided up, that would reverberate throughout Nin's life and her fiction. Later on, I will discuss in a bit more detail the unacknowledged influence Nin had on Duras, but the act of mythologizing a place, unrooting it from physical geography is something Duras also borrowed from Nin, most notably in *The Vice Consul* where both Lahore and Calcutta are situated by Duras within a day's walk from one another and also in her books *Le ravissement de Lol V. Stein* and *L'Amour,* where the name of the town that comprises the mise-en-scene is called first S. Tahla and then S. Thala.

Here is how Nin describes her first look at June, from the unedited diary *Henry and June:* "A startlingly white face, burning eyes. June Mansfield, Henry's wife. As she came toward me from the darkness of my garden into the light of the door I saw for the first time the most beautiful woman on earth."[14]

---

13. Nin, *The Diary of Anaïs Nin, Volume IV, 1944-1947* (n.p.: Harcourt Brace Jovanovich, 1971), 225.
14. Nin, *Henry and June: from the Unexpurgated Diary of Anaïs Nin* (n.p.: Harcourt Brace Jovanovich, 1986), 14.

Smitten, she goes on to say, "By the end of the evening I was like a man, terribly in love with her face and body, which promised so much, and I hated the self created in her by others."

Thirty years later, when Nin is selecting and editing her diaries for publication, the encounter is expanded upon in a paragraph that appears between these two passages: "By the end of the evening I had extricated myself from her power. She killed my admiration by her talk...the enormous ego, false, weak, posturing."[15]

And in the closing passage quoted above, she edits herself back from the brink: Rather than saying "I was like a man" she instead declares (much less boldly) "I felt as Henry did.": "By the end of the evening I felt as Henry did, fascinated with her face and body which promises so much, but hating her invented self which hides the true one."

If in her edited version, Nin seems to think June invents lies about herself, in the intervening fictional accounts of the same meeting, she still feels it is others, including Henry and herself, who project their desires onto June.

Nin made her first attempt at creating fiction from this impactful meeting in the story "Djuna" from her second book of fiction *The Winter of Artifice*. This book was originally published in France in 1939 as part of very small series that also included books by Lawrence Durrell and Henry Miller. Most of the copies disappeared when Nin and other American nationals left France that same year. When Nin reprinted the book (as *Winter of Artifice*) she took the story "Djuna" out and included revised versions of the other stories. In this long-lost story Nin writes of her meeting June Miller: "As she walked heavily toward me from the darkness of the garden into the

---

15. Nin, *Diary, Vol. 1*, 20.

light of the doorway, I saw for the first time the woman I had always been hungry to know. I saw Johanna's eyes burning. I heard her voice rusty and tragic saying: 'I wanted to see you alone,' and immediately felt drowned by her beauty, felt that I would do anything Johanna might ask of me."[16]

She goes on to confess that she wanted to tell Johanna, "'I recognize you. I have often imagined a woman like you.' But I was too timid and instead I sat silent in the tall black armchair."

Like Judith Sands in *Collages*, here Djuna, a stand-in for Anaïs Nin, comes face to face with a woman she has imagined. How much of Djuna's love for Johanna, or Nin's love for June Miller was a self-created thing? Djuna loves Johanna a long time before she finally meets her. She confesses, "The only thing I do not tell Hans is that I too am a Johanna."

"Djuna" along with the rest of the original *The Winter of Artifice* was finally reprinted in 2007. When Nin arrived in New York and republished *Winter of Artifice* (minus the "the"), she did not include this novella. She took some of the material to insert in *Ladders to Fire*, assigning some of Johanna's attributes to the character Sabina, who was further expanded when in later editions of *House of Incest* the character of Alraune is also transformed into Sabina.

Even the material she kept, she once again worked to diminish the intensity of. Here is the same passage above as it appears in the later novel *Ladders to Fire*: "As she walked heavily toward Lillian from the darkness of the hallway into the light of the door, Lillian saw for the first time the woman she had always wanted to know. She saw Sabina's eyes burning, heard her voice so rusty and immediately felt drowned in her beauty. She wanted to say: I recognized you. I have often imagined a woman like you."[17]

---

16. Nin, *The Winter of Artifice: a facsimile of the original 1939 Paris edition*, (n.p.: Sky Blue Press, 2007), 67.
17. Nin, *Cities*, 90.

Not only are we no longer in the garden, but we are also out of the first person and into a fictional third person. The protagonist of the scene is the no-longer very autobiographical Djuna but instead the—according to Nin—completely fictional Lillian. We are placed at a remove but it is a remove that allows a bravery: rather than Djuna's equivocation to Johanna at the end of the earlier version of the passage Lillian is actually later able to tell Sabina that she is a creature of Lillian's previous imagining.

Nin's major concern here and elsewhere—are we only loving one's self in the other?—led her in earlier writings to criticize homosexuality and lesbianism, most pointedly in the characters of Michael and Donald from her book *Children of the Albatross*, but also in the story "Djuna," in exploring the relationship between Djuna and Johanna.

The issue of whether we only love the self in the other is treated with perhaps greater depth and subtlety and sensitivity in her earliest book of fiction, *House of Incest*, because it is explored without the potentially troublesome metaphor of homosexuality. It's also worth saying that Donald has a better, stronger and more functional relationship with Sabina, who seems to see him as an equal and a comrade, rather than with Djuna, who sees him nearly as a romantic rival, or at least as a rival for intimacy.

Here another version of the scene in the garden, from *The House of Incest*, now described in highly lyrical language, nearly poetry and though poetry, closer than any of her explicitly sexual writings to pornography: "Alraune's face was suspended in the darkness of the garden. From the eyes a simoun wind shriveled the leaves and turned the earth over; all things which had run a vertical course now turned in circles, round the face, HER face. She stared with such an ancient stare, heavy, luxuriant centuries flickering in deep processions. From her nacreous skin perfumes spiraled like incense...A voice that had traversed the centuries, so heavy it broke what it touched, so heavy I feared it would ring in me with eternal resonance; a voice rusty with the sound of curses and the hoarse cries that issue from the delta in the last paroxysm of orgasm."[18]

Alraune, eleven years later re-christened Sabina by Nin when she re-published the book in America, is hardly even human here but a seductress of mythic proportions. June Miller, ever the trickster, changes names and bodies, linked by retroactivity to the other novels of Nin's in which Sabina—and this very scene—reappear. Nin decided to change the name when she learned from Otto Rank the connotations of the name "Alraune," that the word also meant "witch" or "sorceress." You see, even though Nin was exploring archetypal implications of her characters with their tendencies toward acting out certain perspectival dramas, she was still committed to depicting holistic women. Nin's humorous but dismissive response to Marguerite Duras' reduction of Sabina into a whore archetype in her (so far) unseen film treatment of *Spy in the House of Love* bears this out.

But in the psychic space of the *House of Incest*, as opposed to the real physical houses of the later encounters, Alraune's relationship to the nameless narrator is more directly and unproblematically viewed. "I AM THE OTHER FACE OF YOU," the narrator declares. "THIS IS THE BOOK YOU WROTE/AND YOU ARE THE WOMAN/I AM."[19]

The embracing of fluidity between people, between the self and the other, between Johanna and Sabina, between Sabina and Alraune, between Sabina and the later Djuna, between the first Djuna and Lillian, seems all essential to the move also between diary and fiction.

---

18. Nin, *House,* 14-15.
19. Ibid., 22.

Our natural inclination is to plumb the depths of the diaries to find the secret seeds of the fiction but it works the other way as well—to see the diaries as extensions, as further constructed works that themselves are another tool for seeing the self.

In answer to any criticism, Nin herself wrote in impassioned outburst, "Your lies are not lies, Alraune. They are arrows flung out from your orbit by the strength of your fantasy. To nourish illusion. To destroy reality. I will help you: it is I who will invent lies for you and with them we will traverse the world."[20]

But like the nineteenth-century deep-sea diver with his hose of air connecting him to the ship, she further writes, "But behind our lies I am dropping Ariadne's golden thread—for the greatest of all joys is to be able to retrace one's lies, to return to the source and sleep for one night a year washed of all superstructures."

She walks into the house of her book to save herself. Into the house of the diary to find the missing room.

In the sinister house of loving only the self in the other, she sought to excavate the sealed up well and fountain. In the "sealed room" she thought she might find her missing other, her missing brother.

Never before could she flow freely. Always she was a ship "choked in its own sails."[21]

Only until she moved to California and built an open house, a house without rooms, could she look out into space and see the waters.

In this open house away from New York City, Nin is about write new kinds of novels, ones in which the structure opens

---

20. Ibid., 20.
21. Ibid., 13.

in space, ranges across geography.

From the claustrophobic, hemmed-in cityscapes of *Ladders to Fire,* the walled-in garden and asylum and apartments of *Children of the Albatross* and the houseboat-bound *Four-Chambered Heart,* Nin transitions through *Spy in the House of Love,* which ranges from the steel and stone canyons of New York City to the sun-filled beaches of Long Island, to be able to write the story of Lillian finally facing down her demons in *Seduction of the Minotaur,* and then later to write a very different kind of novel, *Collages,* which travels from Mexico to California to Turkey and back.

Collages is not only a geographically open book, but it has a most experimental and postmodern structure, told in little episodes. Also, unlike any of her earlier books, it includes a wide range of supporting characters with no real "main character" unless you include Renate, but she herself moves in and out of the book frequently.

As the characters from *Children of the Albatross,* Renate moves on and off stage without necessary import for the plot, but rather like a dancer making her entrances and exits. Houses with their closed quarters and elaborately choreographed stage sets give way to wide open spaces, sparsely but evocatively furnished life a stage for dance.

Dance

In the house of incest, where one only loves the self in others, in the secret room, among paintings and museum objects, lonely wanderers arrive.

Not in the modern Christ, nor in the paralytic nor in the missing brother do they see any chance for liberation from their imprisonment, but in the dancer who dances "the dance of the woman without arms."[1]

She dances to music that no one can hear. She is dancing the dance of a woman whose arms were taken away from her as punishment because she "clutched at the lovely moments" of life, her "hands closed upon every full hour."[2]

Upon the end of the dance, the dancer seems shocked she still has arms, though still "she relinquished and forgave, opening her arms and her hands, permitting all things to flow away and beyond her."

There is always a tension between the "choking" up of the

---

1. Nin, *House,* 50.
2. Ibid., 51.

narrator and the ability of the dancer to allow things to flow to, through, and away from her own self.

Djuna from the original *The Winter of Artifice,* disappeared in the opening days of the world war, refracts herself into real fiction—into Lillian (Nin's declaration of Lillian as pure fiction notwithstanding), into Sabina and also into a new Djuna, who appears in an early state in the new *Winter of Artifice* and then in the *Cities of the Interior* novels.

How much richer it would be to think of Nin's "characters" the way characters are thought of in a dance or ballet rather than the way characters are thought of in theater or in fiction.

A character's role in a dance is by gesture and affect. They interact and behave with others on the stage of action to make visual impact. Their power is in their body, or in Nin's case in their psychic affect.

You can imagine it clearly if you have seen a *butoh* performance, its sources not physical but from inner emotions, the dancer's face the most important point of communication, the enactment of feeling and spiritual need more important than showmanship or athleticism. Kazuko Sugisaki, one of Nin's translators, discusses Japanese Noh drama as an analog to Nin's novels: "The *noh* stage is only eighteen feet square, with its own roof within the theater building, supported by four pillars. No elaborate settings and backdrops are required; there is nothing but a stylized pine tree painted on the boards at the back of the stage. Hardly any props are used: an open framework of bamboo can represent a boat, or a wagon. If a house is needed, a simple structure of four posts with a thin roof will do."[3]

---

3. Kazuko Sugisaki, "Staging the Dream: Japanese Noh Theater and the fiction of Anaïs Nin" in *Anaïs Nin: An International Journal* vol. 6, ed. Gunther Stuhlmann, 1988, 79.

This spare arrangement suggests Nin's sets, which veer away from "realism" and more toward poetic "reality." While Nin talks of being criticized by a reviewer who suggests that her character Stella is unrealistic because she never goes to the icebox for a snack, she suggests rather that a novel lacking the inner reality of its characters is the false one. Life, Nin posits, is governed by dreams and its subtleties are not often adequately depicted by the concept of plot as it is commonly understood. As Sugisaki further says about a Noh play, "There are no quick, exaggerated movements [in the dance.]..." "the audience is almost unaware when a movement begins or when it changes."[4]

Novels like this become performances in a way, with characters that could be played by anyone, the writer or the reader.

Alraune becomes Sabina. Isolina becomes Jeanne and appears again in the story "Under the Glass Bell."

It's not a one-to-one transference because Johanna also became Sabina and Djuna refracts into a new Djuna and transmutes herself again.

Years later, Nin would meet Renate Druks in California and realize sometimes the character is written first and the dancer appears who is perfect for the role.

"All the various women may converge into one," Nin wrote in her Diary while writing *Children of the Albatross,* "because down deep, in the unconscious, there are resemblances... There are exchanges, interchanges, and convergences, and parts of ourselves pass into others."[5]

As Sugisaki explained about the characters in Noh, "The

---
4. Ibid., 82.
5. Nin, *Diary, Vol. IV,* 140.

number of actors on the stage is limited, and very often the *shite,* or 'doer' dominates the entire stage," and that this ritualized approach to performance can "draw the audience into an orbit where art can travel freely across the border between the conscious and the unconscious, between everyday reality and the dream."[6]

And in fact, like the conclusion of Nin's *Children of the Albatross, Winter of Artifice,* and to an extent *Seduction of the Minotaur,* portions of the play can even depart from "reality" entirely: "The second act of "Izutsu" takes place entirely in the priest's dream."[7] Nin, a Piscean water sign, created her trio of heroines to represent various archetypes, including the elements, though each inflected with the other—for Lillian, earth; for Sabina, fire; and for Djuna, air.

As the cycle of novels continues, each woman is challenged by the next element in the cycle: Lillian confronts fire in the climactic motions of *Ladders to Fire,* Sabina the fire-bird must contend with the buffeting and stormy forces of air in the closing scenes of *A Spy in the House of Love,* and Djuna battles the element of water in the form of a dangerous leak in her houseboat at the end of *Four-Chambered Heart.*

The four elements meet when Lillian travels to Golconda in *Solar Barque/Seduction of the Minotaur.*

In the case of *Children of the Albatross,* Nin not only uses dance as a subject matter for the novel but also uses the structure of dance to construct it. "Paul had tremendous fears, of life, love, art, everything," she writes of one of the characters. "I used the wordless language of the ballet to be able to render his timidities, his swift exits, his evasions, his pirouettes."[8]

---

6. Sugisaki, "Staging the Dream," 82.
7. Ibid., 81.
8. Nin, *Novel of the Future,* 124.

Children of the Albatross has three general "movements," or sections. As in an evening-length dance work, each tells a separate part of the story, and separate rhythm of language and kinetic movement.

The first two movements are included in the chapter "The Sealed Room," the title of which refers again to the secret room deep within the mythical house, in this case described with language from the *Diary* as Djuna's house in the suburbs of Paris; this chapter is primarily concerned with Djuna and her attempts to find love and affection and fulfillment after a childhood of alienation, at least part of it spent in an orphanage. The third and final movement is the second chapter "The Café," which re-introduces the other characters from *Ladders to Fire,* including Lillian, Jay, Sabina, and Faustin, and also concludes the stories of Djuna, Michael and Donald begun in the earlier part of the novel.

This movement, "The Café," is sort of a hinge moment in *Cities of the Interior.* Though it is not half-way through the work, it does provide a conceptual turning point. It is followed by three novels, *Four-Chambered Heart, A Spy in the House of Love* and *Solar Barque,* which concern themselves with a single individual character—Djuna, Sabina, and Lillian respectively. Gone are the interactions between the three women (though Sabina does appear briefly and crucially in *Four-Chambered Heart* and Djuna returns the favor in *Spy in the House of Love*) and the large ensemble cast that characterized the first two novels of the sequence; they do not return until the long, extended coda that Nin wrote to *Solar Barque* when she re-published the book as *Seduction of the Minotaur.*

Whereas *Solar Barque* ended with Lillian still in Mexico, in the moment of alchemical transformation, *Seduction of the Minotaur* deals with the aftermath of the climactic events of Lillian's last days in Mexico and then ends on her journey home while she is still en route, high up in the air.

"Home" being an up-in-the-air, porous place—because though *Children of the Albatross* and *Four-Chambered Heart* do take place specifically in Paris, and *A Spy in the House of Love* takes place in New York City, until Lillian's sensual and immediate interaction with the ironically mythical landscape of Golconda in *Solar Barque,* the books as a whole have a more mythically placeless feel about them and at any rate the characters are all together wherever they are. In a way, "Paris" and "New York" feel a little like stage-sets the character-dancers are inhabiting.

Lillian's moment in of rootedness in *Solar Barque* evaporates in the coda which takes place internally in her mind as she flies home. The book ends in the dream.

In *Children of the Albatross,* dance is a way out for Djuna. After a childhood of crutches and pain, she "discovered the air, space and the lightness of her own nature."[9]

How different this is from the weighed down narrator of *House of Incest* who declares, "I am the most tired woman in the world...I need to put something heavy like that on top of my head...I know that I am dead."[10]

For Djuna, "at the moment of dancing a fusion took place, a welding, a wholeness. The cut in the middle of her body healed, and she was all one woman moving."[11] This search for wholeness characterizes Nin's work as a whole but in particular it explains why she engaged with the same characters over and over again through a series of novels, short stories and novellas. Nin commented, "The diary taught me there is interest in development and growth. These cannot be telescoped in one novel if the character itself is rich, interesting or adventurous."[12]

9. Nin, *Cities*, 142.
10. Nin, *House,* 13.
11. Nin, *Cities*, 142.
12. Nin, *Novel of the Future*, 64.

Years after she had completed the *Cities of the Interior* cycle she nonetheless commented, "Sabina is not finished, nor Djuna. I'm working on completing them all."[13]

In Djuna's case, dance also brings her material independence and provides the milieu for symbolic sexual liberation: after the dance class, the ballet master approaches her, bends on one knee, lifts her skirt and kisses her "at the core."[14]

She cannot succeed until she confronts her own issues of abandonment. "I cannot dance, live, love as easily as others," she wishes she could tell him when he asks her to go away with him to dance. She worries she would have an accident, break her leg: "Because this inner break is invisible and unconvincing to others, I would not rest until I had broken something for everyone to see."[15]

Understanding then that the real wound is internal rather than external, Djuna moves back into her memories of growing up in the orphanage, surviving by flirting with the Watchman, finally making it out and on her own to her house in the suburbs.

Her first actions are to unearth the well, unseal the fountain to let the water flow.

Lyrical and poetically, Djuna lives, but she knows in her heart, "each time she walked, muffled, protected, she was aware of two young women walking: one intent on creating trap doors of evasion, the other wishing someone might find the entrance that she might not be so alone."[16] In this way she echoes the earlier actions of Jeanne's brother in *House of Incest*.

---

13. Nin, *The Diary of Anaïs Nin, Volume V, 1947-1955* (n.p.: Harcourt Brace Jovanovich, 1974), 129.
14. Nin, *Cities*, 134.
15. Ibid., 135.
16. Ibid., 148.

Imperfect love follows. Will she love only the self in the other?

Enter Michael who is other face of her, who matches her poetry and her airy nature, able to enter "the flowered regions behind the forts" of Djuna's defenses.

Michael and Djuna's *pas de deux* ends, perhaps predictably, when Michael moves away from Djuna and toward his "succession of Donalds."

But it's Donald, the young gay man whom Michael becomes involved with, who preoccupies Djuna, playing the role she sees as hers, the "feminine" role, but without Djuna's need for evasions and deceptions. Djuna envies Donald's ability to embrace his own nature and evade the social constriction that she still feels bound by.

Always self-perceptive, Djuna sees Donald as more truthful, thinking "how openly Donald betrayed he did not love Michael, whereas she might have sought a hundred oblique routes to soften this truth." Michael on the other hand, thinks "Donald is more truthful because he loves less."[17]

Their distance, their "ballet of unreality and unpossession," dissolves from narrative to lyric, from the third person narration to a first person monologue—"When will I stop loving these airy young men who move in a realm like the realm of the birds…"—and from the language of poetic fiction to the language of science.

From the scene in the café with Djuna, Michael, and Donald, the opening movement finishes with the famously odd passage drawn from a lecture of a nameless research scientist that interrupts the narrative to discuss in technical and scientific terms the mechanics of breath in a bird's body and how it

---

17. Ibid., 159.

allows flight.[18] This shift in diction mirrors the emotional distance that has entered Djuna's relationship with Michael and, as in sculpture or collage, gives a texture and physicality to the writing.

The heart of the novel, the plot that gives it its name, is the middle movement, the tale of Djuna as an older woman, living in an apartment in the city. She develops intense friendships with much younger men—Paul and Lawrence among them.

Eventually her relationship with the seventeen-year-old Paul is consummated. In a tenderly sad scene, Djuna moves toward a vase of tulips on the table. Petal by petal, she opens the closed tulips. From the bed Paul cries out, "Don't do that!"

Heartbroken, Djuna realizes "she opened him to love too soon."[19]

Young Paul longs to stay with Djuna but his family conspires to draw him away and eventually he does leave her. Denied the clean break of a more traditionally tragic ending, Paul must bring back to Djuna the clothes he wore in her presence as his mother will not launder them in her house: "The smallness of his shirts hurt her."

Their last night together they lie in bed and listen to Franck's Symphony in D.

The music, which she heard first at sixteen—close to Paul's age at that moment—takes her back through her failed relationships.

It reminds her of a story she heard of a woman named Matilda who had been asked to wait by the quay by her lover who then abandoned her and never returned. Matilda stayed there, year

---
18. Ibid., 160.
19. Ibid., 181.

after year, going crazy.

"Matilda had been mercifully arrested and suspended in time, and rendered unconscious of pain. But not Djuna."[20]

She sees now, in the closing motions of the second movement, her romance with Paul, how her life had always been "a ballet of oscillations, peripheral entrances and exits, figures designed to become invisible in moments of danger, pirouetting with all the winged knowledge of birds to avoid collision."[21]

Notes of choreography for a novel-as-dance.

And suddenly then on the stage, in "The Café," comes the whole company of dancers, crashing around Djuna, whose—until that moment—this novel had been.

The chapter is made of short little vignettes, each of them describing a single character or characters on an evening before they arrive at the café. These scenes prefigure the larger structure of *Spy in the House of Love* where the episodes are spatial rather than temporal, all happening at once, in different places scattered throughout the city.

Sabina. Jay and Lillian. Faustin. Philip. Michael and Donald. Even Rango, who will not appear as a fully drawn character until *Four-Chambered Heart*, is mentioned. All of the personalities together comprise a context of relationships in which Djuna negotiates her own identity.

While shopping on the street on the way to the café, Michael finds a rare book on astronomy. Donald finds a music box with no actual box, only the spiny music-making mechanism.

While Donald refuses to share his music, Michael dreams

---
20. Ibid., 196.
21. Ibid., 197.

of connection. Donald buys a bunch of emerald balloons, hoping to be borne aloft and when disappointed, releases the balloons, watching "their ascension with delight, as if part of himself were attached to them and were now swinging in space."

The buoyancy that both Michael and Djuna dreamed of isn't to be. And amid the crowded café scene, full of noise and crazy talk, the organ grinder playing, his dancing monkey performing, when Michael asks about Paul, Djuna suddenly turns away, "back again into her labyrinthian cities of the interior."

The stage empties, or rather the lights lower and soon only Djuna is seen, alone on the stage as the other dancers creep off in the half-light.

Her soft motions, the houses and birds and streets she sees, are but reflections of internal states, she is left alone then at the end of the dance with herself. Here people are not distinct personalities but instead "lost their identities to better be carried and swept back and forth through the years to find only the points of ecstasy."

Paul has disappeared; Djuna's house has disappeared. She drifts in an interior state, from this novel into the next, where she will be living adrift—on board a houseboat.

The qualities of dance that formally govern the structure of *Children of the Albatross* appeared a little earlier in the closing party scene of *Ladders to Fire*.

That closing scene, is told not from the perspective of Lillian, the protagonist of the novel so far, but from that of the Chess Player, a new character.

Like Clarissa Dalloway's party, it is one where most of what happens is under the surface; also like Clarissa's party, the narrative awareness shifts away from the main character Lillian—from the Chess Player to Sabina to Lillian, back to the Chess Player, and finally, in the climactic moment, to Djuna.

The Chess Player is so called because he makes a game out of moving participants around the room, manipulating them into encounters with each other. Unlike other nameless male entities in Nin's fiction, for example The Voice and The Lie Detector, The Chess Player does not seem to be aware of the qualities of the personages he is interacting with but his own agenda is not personal nor motivated by personal growth but rather he is fulfilling the obligations of his nameless role.

Lillian, Sabina, Jay and Djuna once more have the affect of characters in a dance, interacting with one another from their basic motivational constructions, like the Noh dancers given foundational movement vocabularies.

In Djuna's case, as seems always, her fear is loneliness. She tries to break free from the Chess Player's strictures, by joining another person on their square, but she is "captured," sent off with one of Jay's "winey, white-trash friends," carried off to "the dark room of her adolescence."

As she disappears from the stage in *Ladders to Fire,* she must change costumes quickly to prepare for her entrance on the very next page—the opening of *Children of the Albatross*: "Stepping off the bus at Montmartre, Djuna arrived."[22]

The moment her foot touches the ground, the whole place erupts in action and music.

---

22. Ibid., 128.

A Design for a Choreography:
Children of the Albatross

Stage Set:

First Act:

A street scene stage right. A dance studio stage left. These are separated by some form of boundary, a curtain, a row of boxes, or flowers strewn on the floor. Movements in the studio are ritual and held postures. Movement on the street should be natural, unrehearsed. Djuna solo, on the street. Duet in the studio, Djuana and the dance instructor.

When Djuna begins to remember, the boundary should be removed. The stage is bare for the memories of the asylum and her house. Duet Djuna and watchman. Djuna solo. Trio Djuna, Michael, Donald.

Second Act:

Djuna's apartment. A low and large area to upper stage left for Djuna's bed. Can be conceptual: the floor covered in a white sheet, as in Duras' *Malady of Death*. A set of wooden bars should hang low to create a vertical boundary, some sense of feeling closed in. Paul will hang his bird from this rafter. Djuna solo. Duet Paul and Lawrence. Trio of Djuna, Paul, Lawrence. Duet Djuna and Paul.

Third Act:

The café. Lillian and Jay's apartment. A street scene for Michael and Donald to walk through. A barricaded area for Faustin. All stage sets should be present at once. The characters will walk through and among each other. For example, Lillian and Jay may be lying in bed while Michael and Donald are at the book stall. Characters should not enter and exit during the third act but remain where they are, joining together in the café when Djuna arrives. Duet Lillian and Jay. Duet Michael and Donald. Faustin solo. Djuna solo.

Characters:

Dancing roles: Djuna. The dance instructor. The watchman. Paul. Lawrence. Michael. Donald. Lillian. Jay. Faustin.

Non-dancing roles: The detective. The scientist.

Music:

Organ-grinder music, "Carmen." Debussy, "Ile Joyeuse." Franck: "Sympony in D."

First Act:

Djuna enters. When her foot hits the stage, all the lights and music from "Carmen" come up. Ensemble moves around her in ordinary street activity.

With her arms open, Djuna moves through the street. Still and small movements, jerky movements. Djuna's fear: if she loved someone, she would break.

Djuna enters the studio. The dance instructor takes her and dances a strong and athletic dance with much ritual sexual, but in a beautiful way, like a tango. Held postures. Djuna is pliable, soft. A passive partner. She loves him but must deny him.

When she leaves him, the barrier is swept away. Ensemble retreats. Djuna alone in the darkened stage. The watchman hovering at the edge of the spotlight in the dark.

Djuna dances softly in the center of the light. Debussy. A child's movements, soft and innocent, not yet realized.

The watchman swoops in. As with the dance instructor, Djuna dances passively, guided and manipulated by his movements. Not like the dance instructor, more carnal, violent. Not manipulating her for beauty but for his own use. Eventually she releases herself from him, but she comes back. She releases herself, she comes back.

When Djuna learns to dance even when bound by him, he melts off her, retreats in the dark.

Djuna's house.

Finally Djuna will move fluidly, under her own power. Incorporate the groundedness of the house with the sprightly fountain. Element of air brought out by the various moods of the house, the colors. A swatch of rose fabric for Djuna to dance with. A swatch of yellow, swatch of brown.

Enter Michael with Djuna. As a bird. Surrounding her, loving her but unable to be touched. She reaches for him but cannot have him. Enter Donald. As a bird. She wants him also but cannot have him.

Debussy. And the research scientist slowly reading over it: "Birds live their lives with an intensity as vivid as their colors..."

Djuna falters into her own slower and internal movement while Michael and Donald take athletic leaps around her.

Second Act:

Djuna's apartment.

Djuna soft, alone. Movements recalling movements from the house but with slower pace and greater deliberation. Enter Paul and Lawrence with great athletic leaps and joys. While Djuna is still in the center, they play their games. Physical dance. Battle with measuring-tape swords. Paul lifts Djuna to tie the bird to the rafter of the apartment.

Djuna and Paul retreat to the area of the bed. Lie in the bed, sometimes covered in sheets sometimes not. They dance in contact with each other always, horizontal always.

Djuna rises from the tangle of sheets to go to the flowers. She begins opening the tulips. "Don't!" cries out Paul. "Don't!"

Music: Franck. Symphony in D.

Paul and Djuna dance together, tenderly. They will say good bye to each other's bodies. A dance like the last sexual experience, touching each other in different places, wanting to remember. Touches lingering. Djuna finally becomes a dominant partner, manipulating a passive Paul the way she was manipulated earlier, but very differently, tenderly, gently, though just as erotic.

Paul pulls away from Djuna, leaving her then, in the dark.

Third Act:

All activity simultaneous.

Music: Organ-grinder's "Carmen."

Lillian and Jay in their apartment, movements of great humor and passion.

Donald and Michael in the street. Michael fraught and pained, heavy movements. Donald like a child, skipping, joyful—not seeing him. Donald reaches for a hundred balloons. Donald reaching always upward, away from Michael. Michael born down, earthward.

Faustin solo in his enclosure, strange and in the corner, in a very limited space. He will appear like the narrator of the story. He mimics in small gestures the grander gestures of a single person on stage. He should choose a character and mimic that person's movement for a while before transferring to someone else. By the conclusion of the piece he should be mimicking Djuna (see below).

The rest of the dancers (Paul, Lawrence, Dance Instructor, Watchman) act as ensemble, people in the café, doing quotidian actions—serving drinks, sitting at tables, coming and going.

Djuna then enters her "cities of interior." As she dances with the fluidity of water, the others one by one come to forms of stillness. The light goes down slowly, slowly on them while Djuna dances.

Transition while the music goes down, from "Carmen" to the Franck symphony.

Light remains strong on Djuna who continues dancing, and half-strength but fading on Faustin, who also continues to dance though slowing down.

By the end of the piece, the music still playing not fading, even Faustin comes to a still position, though still slightly seen. Djuna slows her movements down and the lights go abruptly down while she is still moving—

Music

Like a theme or overture, Rango is seen very briefly in both the party scene at the end of *Ladders to Fire* and in the café with others at the end of *Children of the Albatross*. In neither novel does he function otherwise—merely by mention and a little description like a series of notes or musical overture that will be expanded upon at the beginning of *Four-Chambered Heart*.

The novel opens, in two paragraphs repeated nearly verbatim from his first introduction as the musician at the party at the end of *Ladders to Fire*, with his "pouring into the honey-colored box the flavors of the open road on which he lived his gypsy life."[1,2]

The promise of Rango's music—his passion, his power, is always counterbalanced by his violence, his unwillingness or inability to move forward and grow.

Music helped Djuna to "fuse" together her "conflicting selves"

---

1. Anaïs Nin, *Cities of the Interior*, with an introduction by Sharon Spencer, (n.p.: Ohio University Press, 1980), 116.
2. Ibid., 241.

at the close of *Children of the Albatross*. Sitting with Paul, wistful at what they know to be the end of their affair, they feel soothed by the Franck symphony and its "dissolution of feeling" and "evasion of violence."[3]

The music stands in for their love affair, ending without "explosion," like her earlier, chaste chaste love affair with Michael, a love affair "without climax."

Franck gives them passion "without the storms of destruction" with his "obsessional return to minor themes" and "endless tranquility."

Of course, all is not well in the symphony. Djuna sees in it a "static groove" that she likens to the walled-in room of her ancient house.

Gazing out the window, caught in the eddies and deadening "gentleness" of the symphony, Djuna begins musing again on the story she was told about Matilda, the woman who waits by the quays.

For the lover suspended in time, the lover who will never arrive.

Djuna likewise is able to use music to try to "cure" Sabina at the end of *A Spy in the House of Love*.

Sabina, caught and flying from one affair to the next, Sabina the woman of fire buffeted by the emotional currents that flow within her, pinioned by her guilt, has been confessing in late night phone calls to a randomly selected man.

He calls himself the Lie Detector, and is unwilling to accept a position as passive recipient of the strange woman's

---

3. Ibid., 196.

confessions. He has the phone call traced by a friend on the police force.

And begins stalking Sabina.

After a novel's worth of conversations and analysis with Sabina, he is unable to cure her of either her crippling guilt or of her philandering ways.

Enter *deus ex machina* in the form of Djuna with a well-chosen piece of music.

One of Beethoven's Quartets—she doesn't say which—"began to tell Sabina, as Djuna could not, of what they both knew for absolute certainty: the continuity of existence and the chain of summits, of elevations by which such continuity is reached. By elevation the consciousness reached, a perpetual movement, transcending death…"

In this way the novels accumulate, one after the other with waves of characters and emotion that occur and recur, sometimes sentences or descriptions are used again verbatim or with slight variation. Like a musical phrase or theme in a symphony, often a scene or piece of description or metaphor from earlier in the novel is played again at the end, but with a different character's point of view.

For example, a long time before Djuna thinks of her life with Rango as a "flood for which no Noah's Ark had ever been provided," Lillian thinks the exactly the same thing about her life with Jay.[4,5]

The five novels of *Cities of the Interior* may perhaps unfold chronologically, but it is not the chronology of linear fiction; rather, it feels like the chronology of music, which

---

4. Ibid., 109.
5. Ibid., 270.

incorporates themes and phrases and movements, repeated sections and bridges.

The Lie Detector, still in his rational world, gestures to Sabina "as if this were a graceful dance of sorrow, rather than the sorrow itself." Seeing her weeping, he cannot fathom that the beauty of the music itself, without words, without intellectual thought, has actually cured her.[6]

Sabina, when she reappears in the coda section of *Solar Barque* (published together with the original novel as *Seduction of the Minotaur*) is no longer a fragmented woman of the Duchamp painting. Rather, she stands for a wholeness that Lillian aspires to, a woman Lillian loves but imperfectly because she wants to add herself to Sabina in order to be whole.

Music always means liberation, either spiritual—the bursting into song of the organ grinder the moment Djuna's foot touches the ground when she disembarks from the bus at the opening of *Children of the Albatros*—or even material— Lillian leaving her husband and the strictures of her classical repertoire behind her to go work as a jazz pianist in a hotel bar in Mexico in *Solar Barque* because "classical music could not contain her improvisations, her tempo, her vehemences."[7]

And rather than narrative foreshadowing, Lillian's first secret clue that Jay is going to hurt her is when he forgets a promise to his pianist neighbor to facilitate the delivery of his new piano—upon Jay's return from the café he sees the two pianos sitting on the street in the pouring rain and even years later laughs at the joke of it all. "It was her piano Jay left out in the rain to be ruined," she realizes.[8]

The denial of music always signals a death of spirit or dreams.

---
6. Ibid., 462.
7. Ibid., 569.
8. Ibid., 52.

In the story "The All-Seeing," a man has a violin nailed to the wall of his kitchen, its strings broken. Similarly, Jeanne (the Isolina of the first edition of *The House of Incest*) watches the strings of her guitar break when she finally recognizes that she has turned her back on her own spiritual growth for the sake of others.

Even the organ-grinder's "Carmen" that played so joyously when Djuna dismounted from the bus comes to be rather ambiguous—at the close of *Children of the Albatross,* she hears it again when she is reminded that Paul has gone to India. It plays again when she kisses Rango for the first time and perhaps there functions as a form of narrative foreshadowing of the difficulties ahead.

Rango, though himself introduced as a guitar-playing hero of the open road, is soon revealed to be a caged man, unable to break free. Their first night on the boat together, when he recounts his history in Guatemala to Djuna, he includes the story of his aunt, a pianist who "let herself die of hunger, playing the piano all through the night."

Debussy's "Ile Joyeuse" also connects characters across books. Djuna listens to it in her apartment and later when Sabina returns from a lover to her faithful husband in *A Spy in the House of Love,* Debussy plays while he closes the windows against the night and lights the lamp.

Nin was surrounded by music of course. Her father was a celebrated concert pianist who toured almost until the very end of his life. Her brother Joaquin Nin-Culmell was also a celebrated composer and professor of music at the University of California. Djuna's lover Rango is a guitarist and Lillian is a jazz pianist.

Her characters can be understood—rather than individual personages—as variations on a theme. Djuna and Djuna.

The until recently unpublished Djuna that appears in the earlier *The Winter of Artifice* doesn't feel the same as the Djuna long understood in the Nin canon who appears in *Cities of the Interior*. In this case, she is unlike Alraune and Sabina, or Isolina and Jeanne, who really all do feel like two different names for the same character and which were changed by Nin in order to develop a musical and psychic continuity from *House of Incest* forward into the other books. The two Djunas, like "The Two Fridas," feel like two distinctly different "versions" of each other. The original Djuna is stronger in her desires, more forthright, and even queerer than the new Djuna—more closely analog to the character of Lillian from *Cities,* though Lillian and Djuna appear together in the story "The Voice," which concludes the newer *Winter of Artifice*. One is reminded of the practice in contemporary American soap operas which, because they continue on for years and decades, have resorted to the action of simply recasting roles with different actors who often bring different aspects and flavors to a character long since established.

The later Djuna, "aviator of language, air force for grounded lives," is at once more cerebral, more intuitive, but at the same time more conflicted, less able to pursue her own desires, trapped by her need for love, paralyzed a little bit by her wounds.

The romance between Lillian and Djuna in *Ladders to Fire* is much more of a platonic, friend romance. It's the romance between Lillian and Sabina throughout the novels, but culminating with a kiss or two near the end of *Seduction of the Minotaur,* that feels closer to the relationship between Djuna and Johanna in *The Winter Artifice*.

Djuna Barnes always claimed the character of Djuna's name was taken from hers, which Nin denied, saying she found the name in a list of Welsh names; in fact, according to Nin, it is a man's name. Later Nin more obviously bases the character of

Judith Sands on Barnes.

Though the meeting between Judith and Renate at the end of *Collages* refracts several times, Nin herself wrote of meeting the painter Renate Druks for the first time and seeing in her a character from her own book. The way Nin earlier saw June, the way early-Djuna sees Johanna, and Lillian sees Sabina. Nin also wrote and spoke of feeling snubbed by Djuna Barnes when she tried to meet her. By staging the meeting of Dr. Mann, Renate and Judith Sands, Nin is perhaps trying to heal her own hurt as well.

Lillian knows she will eventually leave Jay after a miscarried pregnancy, though the real reason for the break-up is not revealed until *Spy in the House of Love*, and is told from Sabina's point of view. Lillian tells her side of the end of their relationship in the long coda section of *Seduction of the Minotaur*. Though she begins to play again, she is not able to connect with the real source of music: "She was not playing to throw music into the blue place, but to reach some climax, some impossible reunion with the piano…she pounded the coffer of the piano as she wanted her own body pounded and shattered."

It is not music alone that can liberate Lillian. While she struggles with the piano recital in *Ladders to Fire*, Djuna's attention wanders toward the garden outside the window. While Lillian's nature "was warring with a piano," Djuna notices that there are three full-length mirrors placed carefully among the bushes and flowers.

"The eyes of the people inside could not bear the nudity of the garden," thinks Djuna, but she knows also it is not merely the individual psyche at stake in Lillian's frenzied playing. She knows if people do not come to understand their inner needs, "it would all erupt in the form of war and revolution."[9]

---

9. Ibid., 67.

In the story "The Voice" from *Winter of Artifice,* Mischa has lost his ability to play the cello. His father had returned from hunting and Mischa saw the blood on his clothes. When later he saw blood on his mother's nightgown, he believed his father had done violence to her and so he struck out at him.

But within the secret there is another secret.

His wounded hand, the story of striking his father, was only the visual manifestation of a deeper and more personal hurt.

When Mischa is able to bring this to light he runs from the analyst's room, exultant: "In the street he did not feel the sea of ice, slush and sleet. The warmth in him was like a fire that would never go out. He was singing."

But revelation upon revelation, another of The Voice's clients, Lilith, has been Mischa's lover. She knows the real reason his hand has stiffened—another psychosomatic reason also grounded in sexuality and so at least metaphorically connected with the blood on the mother's nightgown.

Nin, like Franck, returns always to her "obsession with minor chords."

In an interview with *East West Journal,* she says, "my ideal would be a page of writing which would be like a page of music. There must be a language, a way of expressing things, which bypasses the intellect and goes straight to the emotions. I wanted to evoke the same reaction to writing that I have to music."[10]

In this way Sabina learns from the record, not from the psychological questioning. Critics felt the end of *Spy* too "easy," but in the end that may have been the point. The irony here is that the Lie Detector misunderstands. He sees

---

10. Anaïs Nin, *In Favor of Sensitive Man and Other Essays* (n.p.: Harcourt Brace Jovanovich, 1976), 76.

Sabina's weeping at the music as a clinical problem that can be addressed by accepted psychological therapy when the reality is that Djuna has revealed Sabina to herself.

In these novels, it is not only the language that becomes musical, but the structure of the books, the way they unfold, that imitate musical forms—sonatas, quartets, symphonies.

Edgar Varèse, one of the pioneers of *musique concrète,* created a piece based on Nin's book *House of Incest.* In its atonalities, strange percussion bursts and hypnotic astructural rhythms it seeks to recreate the architecture of that book and house in sound.

At one point, Nin visited the home of Edgar Varèse on MacDougall Street.[11] There in his apartment she would see something that would change the way she thought about the form of the novel: his workspace—"on the music stand there was always a piece of musical notations. They were in a state of revision resembling a collage: all fragments, which he had arranged and rearranged and displaced until they achieved a towering construction. I always looked with delight at these fragments, which were also tacked on the board above his worktable and on the walls because they expressed the very essence of his work and character: they were in a state of flux, mobility, flexibility, always ready to fly into a new metamorphosis, free, obeying no monotonous sequence or order except his own."

Always enamored of classical sounds and structures, Nin now found a new source in the so-called "new music" of Varèse and his student John Cage.

Later, in the clubs of Harlem, Nin was exposed to jazz for the first time. Being not born in America, she questioned whether

---

11. Nin, *Diary, The Diary of Anaïs Nin, Volume III (1939-1944),* ed. Gunther Stuhlmann (n.p.: Harcourt Brace Jovanovich, 1969), 155.

she had access to sources of sound that would be able to imitate its rhythms in language.

After meeting Jack Kerouac in New York and later Allen Ginsberg in California (as he describes it, it was *she* who gave encouragement to him when he began to strip during his famous nude performance of "Howl"), she became interested if not in the sentence structure of jazz then in the architectural designs its improvisations of tune and time afforded.

Lillian leaves behind the suffocating "iron lung" existence in Europe to come to Mexico, abandoning her career as a classical pianist to play jazz at The Black Pearl. She equates the shift in music with a change in her outlook of life as well. When grilled at customs about how long she is staying in Mexico, she thinks, "You had to account for every move, arrival or exit. In the world there was a conspiracy against improvisation. It was only permitted in jazz."[12]

How structured are Lillian's movements in *Solar Barque*—all choreographed, she is taken carefully from place to place by taxi, by bus, by raft across the river. Though she came to Mexico for spontaneity, her life there has none of the fluidity of movement offered to the characters of *Children of the Albatross,* who enter and exit the stage like dancers.

As Lillian left classical music behind for jazz, Nin left the somewhat unified and constructed scheme of *Cities of the Interior* and created something more improvisational, more piecemeal, in her final novel *Collages*.

In a way, the structure of *Collages* finally cracked her life-long writing dilemma: how to edit the *Diary* for publication.

Write it like a piece of music.

---

12. Nin, *Cities of the Interior*, 466.

Fugue-like episodes.

Characters that turn and return.

A continuous flow of narrative. The ultimate *roman à fleuve*.

Themes laid down, left, and then returned to and redeveloped. It suddenly became possible to tell the life. It didn't really matter if characters were left out or fused because "the plots and themes of music, like the plots and themes of our life, never alchemized into words, existed only in a state of music, stirring or numbing, exalting or despairing, but never named."[13]

And like Mischa, Nin knew she could achieve honesty while still keeping the secrets she wanted—and needed—to keep.

Of all the veiling and restraint in the original diaries, the most poignant secret was the one she told readers she had decided to keep: her final years of painful illness. The manuscript of the diary ends, as she intended, in 1974, in a bar in Bali, looking out to the ocean.[14]

She kept two journals in her final years, one she titled "The Book of Pain" and other she called "The Book of Music."

"In music," she wrote, "I feel most deeply the passing of things. But with another note, this image is altered, it moves, it fades, it passes slowly, it melts into another image."[15]

She connects music to a state of transformation, both in mortal life, where "secret notes" escape and return a life to its original rhythms—the rhythm of "our first birth, the ocean"—

---
13. Ibid., 478.
14. Anaïs Nin, *The Diary Of Anaïs Nin, Volume 7 (1966-1974)*, ed. Gunther Stuhlmann (n.p.: Harcourt Brace Jovanovich, 1980), 337.
15. Ibid., 340.

but also a transformation out of the body into immortality.

She dreams of herself dying "in music, into music, with music."[16]

Varèse's "Nocturnal," the piece based on *House of Incest*, begins with sharp horn sounds but soon drops into sharp percussion and voices, chanting, strange and low sounds.

In a dreamscape the wall of sounds surrounds one, inviting one into the silent spaces, as in a labyrinth or dark house.

Single notes sustain themselves over a light and occasional sound, wisps of percussion and strings. The voices return, chanting more clearly this time, "You belong to the night."

Fear and tension built and mount with a deeper tympanic burst, chilling strings and shimmering cymbals.

After another space of silence, the soprano enters, singing "I always rise after the crucifixion."

Mechanical noises and the men's voices return to interrupt her, before she continues, lower, more intense than before, "Perfume and sperm/I have lost my brother." She is lost in the sounds of the men's chorus, rising louder with the strings.

Always cut across then by sudden stillness, sudden spaces.

A woman's voice. Rising men's voices.

The cold, intense strings. Mechanical noises and machines.

Silence. Shirred across the surface of silence twinkling strikes. Of wood and snare drum.

---

16. Ibid., 342.

One moves further into the composition, sustained not by a return in musical theme, but by the voice of the woman, changing always in range, quality and intensity. By the closing motions of the piece, she is singing low and wordlessly as in some of Yoko Ono's early musical compositions.

Even as the voices of the men get louder and more frightening, more insistently filling the rooms of the house, she sings, with or without accompaniment.

As Nin introduced a new language and a new way of using it in her fiction, here Varèse introduces some new instruments: in addition to the typical strings and percussion, musicians play a metal sheet, twigs, knitting needles and sandpaper.

His singers' voices, breathless and intense, are governed by the poetic notes he wrote on the score: asking the chorus to sing "deep in the throat as if from underground," the soloist to sing "as if in a dream" and the percussionist to play the wood block "like a drop of water." Later he asks the singers to sing "with imperceptible attack."

The lyrics themselves from the opening section of *House of Incest* hover delicately against the sound around them, human voices lightly inhabiting the house of sound. Varèse, writes Cou Wen-Chung in the introduction to the score, "realized he was more interested in the vocal and evocative qualities of individual words and phrases than in complete poems."

Finally, at the end of the piece, undeterred by the quivering walls of sound around her, "I kissed his shadow," she sings.

Shadow equals the space sound opens in sense.

Fleeting.

Observable only in the half-light of the mind.

A Symphony
(with Notes by Anaïs Nin)

Dug under the accumulating pile of ash from when the cathedrals lay down and light wrote itself across the sky.

Drawn across the strings how can you, sing blue thread into pools spooling.

Ghost lover rejoin me. Sense me and send me rejoin me.

Last night after June filled with June

Danger the thundering chords that bind you.

A secret, like a flickering flame, a secret room unmapped from which music is heard.

Drenched in the ink from the letters, soaked in it, spattered across my chest and neck, pooling in the hollow of my clavicle.

Disappearance of words, each one a black bird written against the sky. Storm-grey, steel-grey sky. Paris after rain.

Cathedral of rain unspooling blue from the sky. Mark me with rain. Spill all the words.

Is it impossible for me to grow in only one direction?

A thousand hands on a thousand doors and a thousand windows to look. Panes of sky, blue, grey, white. In pieces.

Paris. Pieced through or pierced.

When the building opened like a flower and the grey and white ash drifted north into the city, east across the water, what could have been imagined.

A settling of ash into drifts, drifts against the houses and towns, drifts filling the streets, filling the margins of the page like snow. A letter written on the page in white ink, confessing everything, declaring everything.

More likely a thousand letters, each written on top of the other on the skin of my chest and stomach, the small brush licking me, licking me.

I want to fight your surgical knife with all the occult and magic forces of the world.

Rain rushing down the steps of rue des Eaux for the river. A bronze statue of John the Bapstist, rain and river mixing around his feet.

Who am I. Who I once was or who I wanted to be.

Every day I ask for signs every day I fail to see.

Rubbed the inkstone with the wet brush. Light wash of ink. Crisp letters. Spell out the story of your last desire in every space. Choruses of light and languor.

Soft feathery touch on my skin, ink brush or tongue, sand drizzled over it or ash.

A body lying in the margins of the page or in between the lines, nude and turning, blank as a page, waiting to be marked, touched, written upon.

The novel arbitrarily chooses a moment in time. Frames it. Binds it.

This moment. Late summer, finally cool after weeks of blistering heat. I've opened all the windows. Wind blows through the house, too cool to be comfortable but I am grateful at last to be able to feel it. Outside the white dogwood shakes its long branches in the wind.

How do you linger, what do you hear. The low box in the base of harp that resonates.

What do you hear and the wind raises the little hairs on your bare stomach, you pull your arms skyward, reaching.

Blue and grey and white reaching down in strings and rivulets, wet upon you.

Wet upon you wonder, a picture drawn slick in lines.

Hot summer coming over you, soaked then. Drenched. Fingers tracing the outlines of your clavicle, little lake.

Lake wonder in the twilight. Girls with fireflies in their hair.

In the green garden, shards of silver, light reflecting back.

Shorn after the storm, streets wet with asters and deletions. Rain still ringing in your ears.

Lingering at the bridge, the smell of bread baking.

Writing, too, is a symphony, a ballet, a painting.

Charmed by the sky's seduction.

I lie down, wind on my body or water. Warm in the moment after the storm.

Rain drying on the paving stones. Rain-soaked leaves in drifts along the streets.

Haven't you seen my palm where it's written the twenty-seven stars, lines crossing each other.

I want you to press yourself against me, write this minute into my skin.

From rue des Eaux to the Trocadero Gardens, I run as the sky begins again its overture. On the bridge, in the half-rain a portrait painter sits, waiting.

Will I sit? He asks me, the rain already intensifying its demand, streaking down my face, my neck, into my shirt, along my chest, my wet stomach, down below my waist.

And if there is ash and rain mixed with ink, how will you draw a face or body, quivering in time, a day drenched a person become another.

Paint the rain, I beg him. Paint it on my body with your hands.

Film

Louis and Bebe Barron, composers of music for the Shakespearean sci-fi film *Forbidden Planet,* composed a different sort of music as the soundtrack for Hugo's film *Bells of Atlantis,* based on *House of Incest* and with text from that book in the film.

A shimmering and shivering wash of electronic sounds plays over the opening credits, created with the same font Anaïs used to set the text of *House of Incest* for the Gemor Press editions, thus lacing Hugo's foray into film with Anaïs' own early self-publication career.

The screen fills with the rippling vision of water, reflecting what seems to be a California sky, a palm tree waving in one corner.

Anaïs herself begins reading with deliberation and poetic pace, the opening of *House of Incest:* "My first vision of the world was through water veiled."

Though the vision of water veiled abstract shapes are seen: what might be the façade of a house, the inside of a boat, a woman reclining on a hammock.

The figure swinging in the hammock herself makes a boat-like shape as the music rises in intensity and thundering shimmering of metal fills the soundscape.

It's surreal and retrospectively liberating to see Anaïs, refracted through water, drowning almost, set against the watery landscape of the pool and the California palm trees of the house she shared with her second husband Rupert Pole through the eyes of her New York husband Hugo. The two men never met one another until Nin's death, though Hugo claimed that despite all of Anaïs' efforts he always knew about Rupert. Neither man in the bigamous triangle appeared to mind sharing Anaïs, though Rupert always asked her to leave Hugo and move to California permanently.

The film is the one moment we can see the two men (conceptually at least) meet: A woman raises her arms up and dances, seen only as a shadow behind a screen.

Is she the dancer at the end of *House of Incest* or is she the Modern Christ being crucified? Likely she is both.

"This Atlantis could be found at night by the route of the dream."

Finally an arm, a forearm is seen against the wash of water and sound.

Light. A city beneath the waves. And then: a human face. Or is it only the figurehead of a boat?

She lies beneath the waves. "The terror and joy of murders accomplished in silence."

Crucifixion. A woman climbing then from the water.

Nin herself would appear on film again in Maya Deren's film *Ritual in Transfigured Time*. Like her own film star character Stella, she would feel separated from the image of herself on the screen, separated from the main action, standing off in the bay of the window, looking out into the sunlight. Her figure is half-illuminated, framed first by the doorframe, then by the shapes of yarn that Deren and Rita Christiani are winding around their hands.

Stella herself decamped from the novel *This Hunger* to occupy the space in the new edition of *Winter of Artifice* that Djuna had vacated.

That version of Djuna, the original version, would travel to the screen in 1990 in the form of actress Maria de Medeiros.

Transfixed by her physical and vocal similarities with his wife Anaïs Nin, Rupert Pole attended the cinema every single day the opening week of the film *Henry and June*.[1]

Stella rejected the image of herself on the screen—an artifice.

The more chilling question: what if everyone moving through her daily life was only that: a character played by an actress. How far away from the true living self are we as people?

Renate, meet Renate. Djuna, you are not Djuna.

Unlike Judith Sands who does eventually answer the door when Doctor Mann comes calling at the end of *Collages*, Djuna Barnes never responded to Anaïs' letter. It is a rejection she carried close to her, speaking about it even decades later.

The father left the daughter when she was only eleven.

---

1. Fitch, Noel Riley. *Anaïs: The Erotic Life of Anaïs Nin* (n.p.: Little Brown: 1993), 414.

Later the daughter would call the father back. The same father who panicked upon learning the daughter's first novel bore the title *House of Incest*.

Can our "interior mirror" tell us the truth? And who is that figure there moving in light?

Is that what Anaïs felt, watching June Miller walk toward her from the garden?

YOU ARE THE WOMAN I AM. THIS IS THE BOOK YOU WROTE.

And though her lover Bruno saw her first in person, at a party, he still does not see the real Stella but the "dream of Stella." Sabina and Djuna both see themselves refracted as a multitude of women.

Who is the woman herself? Nin once posed for *Town and Country* in four photographs, one of herself as Lillian, one as Djuna, one as Hedja, one as Stella. They were roles she was playing.

She came to regret taking the photographs as they led everyone to autobiographical readings—an obsession which hasn't quit. The photo of Nin as Hedja, veiled, loomed life-sized next to bookstore displays advertising the second volume of her unexpurgated diaries, *Incest*.

After all, it is not as simple as saying Nin drew from her experiences to make the women. Neither can you simply do the math: June = Sabina, Luise Rainer = Stella, etc.

Rather, like Duchamp's painting, the one Djuna thinks is about her and the one Sabina thinks is about *her*, they are each a woman and women. Each drawing knowledge about herself from similar internal and external sources.

Each woman turning into another. Christiani transforming into Deren as she runs into the water at the conclusion of *Ritual in Transfigured Time*.

You and me as well.

Actors playing roles in *Collages* like: Renate Druks. Jean Varda. Lesley Branch. Jean Tinguely. Djuna Barnes playing Judith Sands, who is another version of Anaïs herself.

The man who became a seal in the novel *Collages* then joining the Unknown Woman of the Seine whom Jeanne's brother loved in *Under a Glass Bell*, the woman who drifts away in her houseboat in *Waste of Timelessness*, the doll floating in the water after the storm in *Four-Chambered Heart*, her face washed clean of features.

The spiral staircase up which Stella retreats to flee from Bruno's phone call. Like Sabina's ladders to fire or Djuna's cities of the interior, but leading only to herself and her own solitude. Her bedroom with its Movie Star bed.

Years later, in Mexico, Lillian will feel a similar frustration: her recurring dream of trying to drag a boat through city streets.

It's art that saves Stella, retreating slowly from the sound of the phone, the sound of Bruno's voice, human interaction. She is "annihilated" by the blues and greens of a film on Atlantis with a soundtrack by Stravinsky. Like a Paul Klee painting, the shimmering color enters her mind and Stella is able to enter her childhood and face down the demons of alienation and abandonment that abound there.

The vision of Stella on the screen, though made of light and air, represented a Stella without possible means of communication. It is the Stella that millions loved. When they send her flowers, Stella whispers, "Flowers for a dead woman."

Luise Rainer herself had read Nin's earlier diaries and begged her to write a story in which "Luise could play June."

Enter Stella.

Stella though begins and ends. Nin uses the novella as an example of endings in fiction—that Stella could not continue past the close of the story. It's curious when you consider that all of Nin's other heroines flow from one novel to another. Even Renate, who does not appear until *Collages*, flows and eddies from one end of that novel to the other...

Stella herself was indeed part of the continuous novel at first until she broke off, a shard of glacier sliding off the iceberg back into the sea...

Because she is bound by her life on the screen, separated from actual existence.

Stella does appear briefly in the party scene at the end of *Ladders to Fire,* but even at that party she is like Nin in her film appearance in Maya Deren's *Ritual of Transfigured Time:* separated from the action, a dark muse, music at the sunlight. Later, she opens the door and invites the main character into the strangely ritualized party, everything artifice, gesture, no human contact possible.

The party from *Ladders to Fire* is like that one: a party which Nin joked few actually attend because each is disconnected from the others by their inner loneliness.

As Djuna is enclosed with Paul in the middle section of *Children of the Albatross,* she will close herself up in the houseboat with Rango for most of *Four-Chambered Heart.* Her counterpart, Helba, locks herself up in her house and does not move from her sickbed.

When the three of them go to the beach—that ultimate of wide open spaces—matters will come to a head—that liminal space which figures so largely in *Spy in the House of Love* and in Marguerite Duras' novel *L'Amour* that she wrote after Nin and her agent turned down the treatment she had written for *Spy*.

Enamored by filmmakers like Henry Jaglom, Luis Buñel, and Jean Cocteau, Nin always thought of her novels' potential to be made into films. In particular, she thought of *A Spy in the House of Love* this way.

It's a curious choice, since in a fashion it is a more experimental narrative than the other novels of *Cities of the Interior. Four-Chambered Heart* offers the cleanest linear narrative (other than the *Solar Barque,* which was nonetheless transformed by the impressionistic and lyrical coda added to it when it was republished as *Seduction of the Minotaur*), while *Children of the Albatross* perhaps offers the greatest dramatic and filmic potential: scenes in the orphanage, in the dance studio, scenes in the apartment with her young lovers, in the cafes at night—indeed the film *Henry and June* uses many of the *mise-en-scenes* of this earlier novel to construct the atmosphere of Nin's Paris in the early '30s.

Spy, on the other hand, stays with a single character throughout, though she is stalked by the Lie Detector, and it is episodic rather than a building narrative. Additionally, the narrative is not linear and in fact moves simultaneously or spatially—a strange choice for a film until you consider Nin's love for impressionistic, lyrical, and surreal films.

More importantly, Nin saw Djuna's story as more "romantic," and Sabina's as more "contemporary." Nin found Djuna's story "focused on one love until its ultimate destruction," and so not as resonant with the audience; Sabina's story was one of the "fragmented loves happening all around us…a phenomenon of our time."²

Like Jaglom's *A Safe Place*, one of Nin's favorite films, *Spy* is comprised in discrete scenes, cut against each other, that move smoothly from the interior to the exterior—both literally and within the character's awareness—meant to create an emotional tone, a picture of Sabina's frenzied reality, her inability to choose, her inability to live.

In Jaglom's film, first we are inside, then outside. Three people lounge in a candle-lit room drinking club soda. A couple dances in their underclothes on the roof of a New York apartment.

The end of a relationship is played out while "A Kiss Is Just A Kiss" gently plays.

Nin went to France to meet with Marguerite Duras, then having just been lauded for her screenplay *Hiroshima Mon Amour*, about writing a screenplay for *Spy in the House Love*. Nin liked her and Duras agreed to write a treatment. When it arrived later in New York, both Nin and her collaborator found it unusable. She seems to have had a sense of humor about it, though later commented that Duras had portrayed Sabina "as a whore."³

Sabina definitely spurred Duras' imagination in some way because the same year she wrote the failed treatment she also wrote and published *Le Ravissement de Lol V. Stein*, the story of a woman who, like Sabina, is dealing with the consequences of her love affair. Duras' novel also includes a Lie Detector-like character, in this case Lol herself, who stands on the street and spies on the secret assignations between Lol's friend Tatiana and her lover, Jacques Hold.

---

2. Nin, *The Diary of Anaïs Nin, Volume 5 (1947-1955)*, ed. Gunther Stuhlmann (n.p.: Harcourt Brace Jovanovich, 1974), 288.
3. Nin, *Diary, Volume 7 (1966-1974)*, 172.

Several years later, Duras published an impressionistic and filmic sequel to *Lol V. Stein,* a novel of a woman on the beach being observed by a man walking—*L'Amour.* A year following, she made a film of it called *La femme du Gange,* in the shooting script, calling the woman "Lol."

Her wandering man shares physical traits—his "glacial blue eyes"—with Philip, the opera singer Sabina meets on the beach of Provincetown.

Like Sabina in Provincetown in *A Spy in the House of Love,* Duras' woman is lying on the beach, her eyes half-closed, slowly drizzling her body with sand.

Duras revisits Nin's iconic scene of a woman, awake but with her eyes closed, lying before an observing man, aware she is being observed but unmoving, in several subsequent novels including *Blue Eyes Black Hair, Malady of Death,* and *The Man Sitting in the Corridor.*

None of Duras' biographers comment on the meeting with Nin, nor whether or not Duras felt Nin to be an influence, but Nin herself was aware of *Le Ravissement de Lol V. Stein.* Though she doesn't seem to have commented on any relationship between Lol and Sabina, she was critical of the novel, saying, "in describing Lol's schizoid state, she caused it to happen to such a degree that Lol was no longer understandable. All communication was broken. Madness to me, in a novel, was like murder...an easy and not quite honorable solution."[4]

When Nin finally makes it to the big screen—ironically, not by fiction but by the real live story of Nin, Miller, and June, the one Nin originally wrote as the story "Djuna"—she will have new life as a writer. All of her books will return to print

---

4. Nin, *The Novel of the Future,* with an introduction by Deirdre Bair, (n.p.: Ohio University Press, 1968), 163.

and she will be introduced to a new generation of readers, including this one.

And finally, the viewer too can be transfixed: frozen in place breathless at the sight of Uma Thurman as June—who can forget that thick, rusty voice, that Brooklyn accent, "Thanks for taking care of Henry, Anaïs; he didn't describe you right..."—walking from the darkness of the garden into the lighted house.

A Spy in the House of Love:
A Film Treatment

But one always wonders what a film of *Spy in the House of Love* could look like.

A man sleeps in a darkened room. Fire burns around him, outside the window. The sheets are rumpled with his restlessness.

Outside the window, fire trucks scream down the street. When the gaze of the camera returns to the bed, the room is calm, still.

The telephone rings. Hello.

Your lies are not lies, Sabina, but arrows flung out from your orbit.

As the man talks his mysterious phone caller, we return to a street scene. The city.

A fire engine rushes by, seen through the window at the front of a bar. Inside the bar from the smoky phone booth emerges Sabina. Uma Thurman.

Friends coalesce around her as the excited conversation continues. Sabina is explaining how Moroccan women use coal-dust to rim their eyes. The street is turning red, not from fire but from the sun.

In the corner, in the shadows, dressed now, the man from the apartment. He watches Sabina. She does not see him.

Later, in the restroom. Sound of the bar through the wall. Laughter.

Sabina's face in the mirror. Gaze lingers across her cheeks, mouth, eyes.

The drape of her dress, her black cape.

Her white neck, the barbarian steel necklace around it.

The camera pulls back to follow Sabina walking. Early, early morning, after dawn. Going back to Alan. 55 Fifth Avenue. Sabina walks down the middle of the street, stepping aside for the occasional cab. Around her, early morning activity: shopkeepers opening their stores, etc.

Sabina's inner monologue over it: *But I am safe. He will be asleep.*

Cut with images of Sabina's previous life in the apartment.

Alan welcomes her and they talk. Sabina lies.

Why am I loved by him? Will he continue to love me? Her internal voice.

Alan folds and puts away Sabina's clothes as she runs water for a bath. Interrupted by moments of Sabina's skin, her nude body, Sabina with other men.

She sinks into the water of the bath. The surface of the water ripples.

Ripples of water. Shards of light. The beach. Provincetown.

Sabina sinks below the surface of the water.

By the ocean now, the brightness of the sun through the window of the New York apartment giving way to the bright sun over the beaches of Provincetown, the noise of the early morning traffic flattening out to the roar of the ocean churning.

Sabina stripping nude and lying down in the wrack line.

Allowing the ocean to flow in and over her, dragging sand across her body.

A man. Walking along the beach. Singing.

Sabina, lying on the beach, the sun drying the water on her skin. Close up view of the water on her skin evaporating, leaving behind salt and sand. Her hands half-buried, lifting sand, drizzling it across her body.

Close view of the crystals of sand following. The singing approaches.

Sabina smiles, turns over to face the sound.

He stops in front of her. His shadow covering the sun. She does not move.

Cut with a scene of the two of them, much later together, he is saying "It was because you were silent I came up to you."

Finally, she stands and speaks, dressing slowly.

They walk along the beach, talking. He turns his gaze—"glacial blue"—upon her.

The two of them then, in the dark of the bar, the Dragon. Sabina climbing the iron ladders slowly from the sea, emerging from the sea into the light.

Seen from above, the sea streaked with the red of sunset.

Sabina in the light.

Emerging from the fiery sunset-colored depth.

Philip and Sabina dancing together in the club as the blues are sung in the background.

Philip kissing another woman. It is another time. Sabina observes from a different place in the bar. Sabina cranes her neck, trying to see the woman's face.

"If she is beautiful," thinks Sabina in that same rusty voice Uma used to portray June Miller, "I will not see him again. If not then I can be the whim, the caprice, the drug, the fever."

The woman is not beautiful. *No streaks of lightning in his ice-blue eyes, but a soft early morning glow.*

The morning glow dissolves then in the silver-light of the moon, Sabina, a younger Sabina, softer, unmarked, taking a moon-bath, lying herself nude in the silver light.

Alan closes the windows. It is another time. New York. Debussy's "Ile Joyeuse."

Sabina moving slowly apart from him. He is always gesturing toward her. She cannot see.

A week later. Evening. Sabina emerges onto the street, waiting for the bus. She rides the bus, smoking a cigarette and jumps out at 64th street, even before the bus has stopped.

Sabina walks through the street in a dark dress.

Philip is there, in his apartment filled with skiing trophies and tin soldiers. An umbrella hanging from the ceiling.

Sabina and Philip. And then she is dressing, leaving.

What has been shown and not shown. As she leaves, cutting back to scenes of their bodies. Naked in the bed. Sabina slips out of the bed. In the bathroom repainting her make-up. Shown always in shards and fragments after the fact. Can refract these scenes in bits and slices throughout the film.

Returning to Alan, who is surprised and glad to see her.

A dance. Music and Sabina dancing with a dark-skinned man. From the corner the Lie Detector is watching her.

Iron bars. Prison bars. He watches Sabina through the bars. Is she in prison or is he?

A man hiding. She sees him in the shadows. Is it Alan, she wonders, suddenly panicked.

She rushes past him.

Another time. At the same club. Mambo and Sabina, their nude bodies. Music of Debussy. Mambo says, "You don't love me."

Sabina slipping away. Seen again by the Lie Detector.

Another time. In Mayan ruins. The earthquake ravaged

streets. Facades of buildings like Di Chirico paintings.

The camera swings wildly around her as she sees a lover's room, the sea. Four walls and a bed. Di Chirico. Magritte. Soundtrack now: Stravinsky's firebird. Sabina's "unerring musical autobiography."

Fireworks. Mercury's orange wings "hurled like javelins into space...the purple vulvas of the night."

Mambo and Sabina at an espionage movie. Sabina looking over her shoulder and around her, thinking she sees Alan in every man. "I am an international spy in the house of love," she thinks to herself.

Sabina surrounded in paper, rising up, reaching in the air for paper umbrellas.

Falling through great sheets of paper, they tear and she falls.

The white light of the screen, the bright paper edge, burns and dissolves into the sun.

Sabina at the crossroads in the beach town. Not Provincetown. A different beach town, a different time. Shown by Sabina's hairstyle or clothing.

A cyclist next to her, also waiting for the light to change. He is markedly younger. The light changes. He asks her the way to the beach.

Across her face the ruins of Guatemala. "I hate ruins," she thinks.

Night. She is walking along the street. She cannot sleep.

All the beach towns she's known flashing through her mind—

Provincetown, Capri, Mallorca, Venice, the Italian Riviera, in the south of France, and in South America…

She is given a lift home. They talk of flowers and exile. She is lulled to sleep by the motions of the car.

Sabina in a telephone booth. She wants to go home. She slides down the side of the booth. A knocking on the door. It is the young cyclist.

He spins the story for her of years during the war in Africa. He sees a woman give birth. A plane crash. He is discontented with the civilian life. The boys are all after him.

"In South America," says Sabina, "the women wear fireflies in their hair."

Sabina and John kiss.

Sabina and John in her beachfront cabin. "When I was being trained," he says, "the first thing they told me: Never look in a dying man's eyes."

"But I know you did," says Sabina. "I can see it in your eyes."

She wants him to tuck her in before he leaves. He tucks her in.

As she is being tucked in, the sheet pulled taut, images of a knife plunging down.

Day time. Alan comes. Sabina cannot focus. She walks down the streets with Alan but turns, now looking for John. When Alan leaves, she looks for John: in the town, in the bars, at the bicycle rental place, at his apartment.

Night falls. She sees the light on in his apartment. He cannot see her. His father is coming. They promise to rendezvous in

New York.

Philip. John. Donald. Jay. Faces and echoes of the voices of men reverberate through Sabina as she walks, seen in images across her body, cut to different scenes with each man. Sabina crossing the street. Basking in the gazes of the policeman, the door man, the clerk at the store.

Now Donald's delicate hands turning a rose, twisting a gentle chain around his wrist. Her hand touches her own barbaric necklace.

Donald unlacing her sandal, taking off her silk wrap.

Sabina, lying back on the couch. Donald stripping in front of her, lithe, small.

"You're sad, Sabina," he says. "Come with me, I have something to show you."

Donald's room of toy cages. Bamboo cages, little adobe houses, bathtubs made of mirrors, birdcages.

Sabina puts *The Firebird* on the phonograph. She opens her arms like wings.

Donald in Sabina's embrace, small Donald being engulfed by Sabina.

Fire surrounding them. She breaks away and lifts the needle from the phonograph. Abruptly. Scratching it.

Another time. Sabina is climbing the stairs with her bag of groceries.

A stained mirror. Her reflection. She is worn. Tired.

A letter from Donald to Sabina. Crumpled paper, crumpled paper umbrellas.

Alan and Sabina at the movie theater.

Sabina placing a needle on a record.

The Firebird. The face of John speeding through the clouds. Mambo saying, "You don't love me."

Sabina, moving, cut, seen from different angles, a multitude of Sabinas. Walking, lying down, trying to speak. Being disrupted. Dispersed.

A wild compass fluctuating. The camera gyrates wildly with different visions of Sabina.

Sabina fractured a thousand ways.

And then. It stops. The music. Scratch of record. Donald's distressed face. Her dress slowly deflating. Her cape slowly settling. She enters Mambo's club. Her vision is brought short when she sees the paintings on the wall.

Jay. Paris. Seven years earlier.

Jay painting Sabina. He paints her in the future. It is the Sabina standing in the doorway of Mambo's club on his earlier canvas. In fragments "to the rhythm of debris." Jay painting Sabina split in a thousand shards.

And then. In the present. She sees him. At a table in Mambo's club. Jay.

They sit and talk, joined by friends. It is the scene from the beginning of the film. The fire trucks race by the window as before.

Jay: "The first time I looked at her I thought: Everything will burn!"

Smoke between them. Jay staring at Sabina. Sabina is explaining about the coal-dust Arabian women use in their eyes.

They are laughing. They each speak to each other but are thinking something else behind the words.

Their Paris life plays silently behind the words behind their words: Lillian and Jay. Sabina and Jay. Lillian leaves Jay. Lillian and Djuna. Djuna and Donald.

The thought of Djuna soothes the fire, the trauma, the memory. Cool Djuna loving her. Vision of water and wind. Djuna touches Sabina's cheek gently, in understanding.

The image of Djuna in her mind manifests as Djuna enters the bar.

The drums cease to play. She sees now the Lie Detector, in the corner, writing in his notebook. "Are you here to arrest me?" she asks him.

Djuna approaches. "I've tried to find you since we left Paris," says Djuna. They talk like only old friends can. Sabina wants Djuna to explain her to the Lie Detector, now that she recognizes him. "My trap doors failed me," Sabina says, desperately.

"Come with me," says Djuna, taking her up to her studio where they once more hear the drumming from Mambo's club.

Djuna does not explain. Puts a record on the phonograph. One of Beethoven's quartets.

The music, not the talk, saves Sabina. The music fills her. She softens, her wings drooping down, her dress deflating. Sabina sinks down to her knees, bending her neck. Her dress like a deflated parachute. A fire-bird fallen from the sky, Sabina weeps.

The Lie Detector enters to room timidly. Djuna sees him but does not stop him. He raises his hands tenderly, moving toward Sabina, whispering to her, trying to comfort her—

She turns from him, looks up at Djuna, her face full of tears, and in her sadness she suddenly and finally *feels*.

Painting

Of all the arts, Nin's metaphors and images depend most upon the plastic and visual and her work is haunted by painting and painters, both characters and actual artists.

Jay. Hans. Renate. Jean Varda. Paul Klee. Marcel Duchamp.

Though light shimmers and moves on Stella's screen, the life that unfolds there is life at a distance. Nin saw always the transformative possibilities of painting and sculpture and her work is saturated with tactile experience of the plastic arts.

Art and the making of art is always developed as a metaphor for personal freedom. In *Children of the Albatross,* the young men who come to Djuna's apartment feel that it is a free and creative space. Paul makes a little bird to hang from Djuna's ceiling while Lawrence dyes the hamster's hair blue.

Similarly destruction of art is the purest of brutalities: in a famous scene from *Four-Chambered Heart,* Rango asks Djuna to burn her books because they represent her life separate from him. Even more brutally, because Djuna reasons the books "had not prepared her for moments such as this," she complies. "All these novels so carefully concealing the truth about character, about the obscurities, the tangles, the mysteries," Djuna rails, "Words words words words and no revelation of the pitfalls, the abysms in which human beings found themselves. Let him burn them all; they deserved their fate."[1]

In her 1946 manifesto "Realism and Reality," Nin writes, "The best way to approach my [writing] is as one regards modern painting. I intend the greater part of my writing to be received directly through the senses, as one receives painting and music...a column can signify more than a whole house... [Brancusi] achieved the closest expression of the flight of a bird by eliminating the wings."[2]

Critic Lloyd Morris elaborates a little further in saying that Nin "is not, in the usual sense, trying to tell a story. Her object is to reveal experience directly. She wishes to immerse readers in that flow of sensibility and reflection from which human beings distill the significance of what they do and suffer."[3]

Both Sabina and Djuna think of themselves as the woman depicted in Duchamp's painting *Nude Descending a Staircase*.

For Djuna, this moment comes just after she and Rango experience their conflict over the primary usefulness of political involvement over art. Rango has just met Djuna's friend Sabina and doesn't like her. Djuna feels like "not one but many Djunas," like "multiple selves grown in various proportions, not singly...not moving in one direction, but composed of multiple juxtapositions revealing endless spirals of character as the earth revealed its strata, an infinite feeling of constellations expanding..."[4]

---
1. Nin, *Cities*, 272.
2. Nin, *The Mystic of Sex: Uncollected Writings, 1931-1974*, ed. Gunther Stuhlmann (Santa Barbara: Capra Press, 1995), 23.
3. Evelyn Hinz, ed., *The Mirror and the Garden: Realism and Reality in the Writings of Anaïs Nin*, (n.p.: Harcourt Brace Jovanovich, 1973), 52.
4. Nin, *Cities*, 343.

Djuna could be describing Nin's entire project in *Cities of the Interior,* her theory of character in those novels and in her fiction in general. Not just "Djuna, meet Djuna" but also "Djuna, meet Sabina." Evans is right, then: the application of the meditation on the painting *does* cause the characters to "blur and overlap in the reader's mind."

Which seems Nin's intent, it now seems almost too obvious to say.

When Sabina at the close of *Spy* is walking home, despondently, feeling like she can't just return to Alan one more time, she thinks of the Duchamp painting, feeling like "eight or ten outlines of the same women, like many multiple exposures of a woman's personality...walking down the stairs in unison." If she went home now, she thinks, "it would be like detaching one of these cut-outs of a woman...a divided woman."[5]

She understands her own need for other lovers as stemming from this feeling of fragmentation: "Each year, just as a tree puts forth a new ring of growth, she should have been able to say: 'Alan, here is a new version of Sabina. Add it to the rest, fuse them well, hold them all at once...or else divided, separated, each image will live a life of its own...'"

The stimulus for Djuna retreating into her "cities of the interior" at the café table at the conclusion of *Children of the Albatross*—Michael's question "Has Paul gone to India yet?"—manifests in the sudden grinding to a halt of the organ music, but is described visually through the monkey's red Turkish cap dropping streetward.

For a surreal and non-narrative fiction, *House of Incest* is soaked in the visual—fish of velvet, lace and organdy, grilled mosque windows, each room of Jeanne's house painted a different color,

---

5. Ibid., 453.

even the chapter headings each have an alchemical symbol. It seems only a short leap to make a film of excerpts from the book, but the real visual synthesis happens when Nin adds a set of photomontages created by Val Telberg to future printings.

"I looked upon a clock to find the truth," she writes of time, the ultimate abstraction, yet what follows is told in visual metaphor: "The hours were passing like ivory chess figures, striking piano notes, and the minutes raced on wires like tin soldiers."[6]

Throughout the novels, visual expressions help to see the subliminal reality: the two pianos in the rain. The mirrors in the garden. The oft-repeated synesthetic line, "the street organ was unwinding *Carmen* from its roll of tinfoil voices." A woman lying on the beach with her eyes closed. A doll floating in the river after the flood, its china face washed clean of its features.

Jay tells a story of his friend, a painter. Peter lived in a bare studio apartment. He tricks the concierge into thinking he is going to win a rich painting prize. She agrees to let the rent slide. While he paints, she camps out in the courtyard. They are great friends while he paints, but when the paper prints the name of the actual winner of the prize, she flies into a rage. Storming his apartment, she sees in horror a body hanging from the ceiling. But what the police cut down is a mannequin of wax, dressed in rags, carefully painted to look like Peter. "After that," says Jay, "his luck turned…he seemed to have killed the self who had been a failure." The reader is fooled because ordinarily the point of Jay's rambling stories are the comic narrative themselves, but here—as in the much later novel *Collages*—the real point is the moment of self-transformation enacted by the painter's own act of creativity.

---

6. Nin, *House*, 41.

Nin's humor was always of the black variety. The artist is a trickster, not really a cad, but always, like Woolf's villager-actors in *Between the Acts*, holding up mirrors in the garden. She completes her "continuous novel" in 1959 (though two years later she would feel inspired to add the coda to the final novel) and in the California sunshine, with a whole group of new friends, she returns to her two earliest fictive forms—the more symbolic narrative of *House of Incest* and the short fiction form of *Under a Glass Bell*—to write her last piece of fiction, *Collages*, which she publishes in 1964 and which critic Philip K. Jason calls her "swan song to fiction."[7]

It is the novel that will give her the technical tools once and for all to begin revising the Diary for publication, which she will begin doing immediately upon completion and spend the nine following years editing six volumes of Diary (the seventh will be completed by Rupert Pole after her death).

Most Nin critics have placed their greatest emphasis on looking at ways that the Diary was the laboratory or genesis for the fiction, but we can understand that the reverse is also true.

Collages is a novel that uses as its structural conceit the visual art of Jean Varda.

Duchamp's painting expressed a neurosis of the fragmented self, but Varda's collage "Women Reconstructing the World" gives Nin a positive model of how the fragment or the shard can be used in service of re-integration.

Rather than concerning itself with a single, main personage, it is the ensemble of sometimes unrelated characters that drives the dramatic action of *Collages*. If *A Spy in the House of Love* is destined for the big screen, then *Collages* would make

---

7. Philip K. Jason, *Anaïs Nin and Her Critics,* (Suffolk: Camden House, 1993), 70.

a wonderful and witty short television series.

Though more experimental in its episodic and non-Aristotelian structure and ambition, *Collages* actually retains a much more mainstream discursive, linear, narrative style than Nin's earlier novels which, while fragmented in terms of plot, very much retained a dramatic structure centered around the development and growth of individual characters.

Ladders to Fire built on and obsessed on a smaller focus of characters, though has moments of digression, for example the sections about Helen. *Children of the Albatross* comes closest to a similar structure as *Collages*—episodes loosely grouped into three acts, though *Collages* does not retain the heightened, ritualistic choreographic feeling of that earlier novel; it feels much more natural and spontaneous as it unfolds. *Four-Chambered Heart, A Spy in the House of Love* and *Solar Barque,* as we already discussed, each fixate on the experiences of a single character, and everyone else revolves around her. In a way, *Collages* is almost a riposte to the later novels of *Cities of the Interior*—it introduces a main character, Renate, then allows her to be the eye around which the hurricane of everyone else's drama turns.

The coda section added to *Solar Barque* of course disrupts the unity of that book and links it to the larger, continuous whole of *Cities of the Interior*. In a way, it is that coda—the recounting of Lillian's journey to wholeness reflecting on her relationships with Jay, Sabina and Djuna—that sets up and makes possible a heroine like Renate.

In the first two episodes, Nin begins telling the story of Renate, a woman who grows up in Vienna, and leaves for Mexico, where she frequents The Black Pearl, the same nightclub Lillian once played at, thus linking the two characters by locale.

In the third vignette, Renate moves to California after a disastrous relationship with Bruce in Mexico. Bruce returns to her and begs for another chance, giving her the gift of many puzzle boxes. Whenever she feels she does not understand him, she is to open a puzzle box and inside will find a story of his past. At first the reader is excited, seeing in this gesture perhaps an analog for Nin and her diary and believing the relationship might be saved. Then a more dramatic and perhaps more truthful thing happens: she reads one of them and decides she cannot face all of his secrets and so burns the boxes.

This destruction of art is not the same as Rango's burning of Djuna's books. It is rather Renate's reaction to reading the story—she is preserving their present relationship by refusing the "conclusion" the texts in the boxes would provide.

As the French consul's wife is later told, "Nothing is ever finished."

Continuing the cleansing by fire, in the next scene Renate visits the Laundromat with all of the sheets and linens of the house "stained with the marks of love" and hears the story of the man who works there, who followed his wife from their native Hungary to California. Bruce disappears from the narrative here and the reader might well assume the relationship is over though one has not been told such.

Always in an episodic narrative what is skipped over is at least as interesting as what is left.

As if the mention of the larger world by the launderer had spurred an interest in landscape, the next vignette tells of the small towns of California spread into the hills away from Malibu. A painter drives out to set up shop and paint inhabitants and sell the paintings. We are not told the painter is Renate in disguise until halfway through the chapter. The story of Raven is narrated in which her pet raven assumes her weaknesses while she takes the bird's strengths.

In the seventh episode, Renate drives the coastal highway and hears another story of transformation—a man who dreams himself turning into a seal. These stories all reinforce the notion of transmutation, and a transmutation by creative practice. Because Renate has spoken of the Black Pearl, Lillian is on the reader's mind and the coda of *Seduction of Minotaur* assumes somewhat of a different valence—in retrospect, Lillian has indeed effected a transformation by her performance of jazz music in the alchemically-inflected Golconda.

Collages also has three rough acts—these first seven episodes that recount Renate's childhood and Europe and then moving and settling in California comprise the first such act. What follows are nine more episodes; rather than organized around a character—Renate—these are spatially unified by their setting—the Paradise Inn, a restaurant and nightclub where Renate works as a hostess. Many characters frequent the Paradise Inn including Varda, Leontine the Haitian dancer, Henri the French chef, Nina the actress, Nobuko, Colonel Tishnar and of course the French Consul's Wife, (based on the British historian Lesley Branch) the beautiful and talented woman who captures Renate's imagination and whose story gives the novel its dramatic and poetic center of gravity. Was Marguerite Duras aware of *Collages* when she wrote and published *The Vice Consul* the following year?

If Lillian, at the completion of *Seduction of the Minotaur,* seems headed home with some sense of wholeness (if not closure), then *Collages* can be seen as the psychic sequel to that book. Unlike Lillian, Renate, who also frequents the Black Pearl when she is in Mexico, decides not to return to Europe. Even after meeting a neurotic and fussy American (whom she seems not to judge at all—a stark contrast from Lillian, Djuna and Sabina all, who are quick to analyze both themselves and others), Renate decides that California is the life for her.

The opening act of *Collages* recounts her transformation. Whereas the other novels end either at the point of frustration or inability to transform (*Ladders to Fire, Children of the Albatross*), or at the instant itself of transformation *(Four-Chambered Heart, A Spy in the House of Love,* the original *Solar Barque),* only *Collages* takes as its germinal opening gesture the story of transformation itself—from the stone statues of Vienna, unable to ever change, to the quick changing figures of California, including the Seal-Man and Raven.

Lillian is not the only character from the earlier novels that Renate seems to embody. As a painter, one can link her to Jay; in fact, she repeats Jay's earlier behavior of locking up her lover and leaving the room. When Bruce, like Lillian in the earlier novel, takes umbrage at being locked in the room, Renate laughs and explains, as Djuna earlier explained to Lillian, that perhaps it was her secret desire to keep Bruce to herself that made her lock him in the room.

The second act of *Collages* introduces the group of people around Renate, illuminating parts of character by creating a more composite-like picture, similar to the narrative strategy employed by Woolf in *Jacob's Room,* or Duras in *The Vice Consul.*

After three episodes telling the stories of Henri, Leontine and Varda, Renate again appears on the scene in a very brief episode in which Varda, the collage artist, admires the lining of her fabulous coat. Without hesitation, Renate takes a pair of large scissors and cuts him a large piece of fabric from the coat to use as collage material. It's an act of generosity of course from one artist—Nin—to another—Varda, the man not the character.

And then suddenly, in the thirteenth episode of the book, unseen since episode four, Bruce is once again with Renate at the Paradise Inn. As in the scattered episodes of *Spy* this helps to build in a certain sense of timelessness or spatial arrangement to episodes of *Collages*. One is hard pressed to read the linearity of the episodes and in a sense this introduces into the text a resistance to being read as a typical narrative novel and reintroduces the concept of seeing the parts simultaneously; rather than passively being *told* a story, the reader must actively experience the episodes "through the senses" as in modern painting, the way Nin intended. Rather than a chain of events, it is a composite series meant to be seen and experienced at once.

Nina the failed actress, Nobuko the aspiring actress, the Consul's wife, and the failed romance of Tessa and the Colonel are then told in a second series of brief episodes, before the "second act" of *Collages* closes with a story of Renate's failure to create a magazine; dreams to create art cannot always compete with material realities.

Hope and potential govern the opening movements of *Collages* and frustration of potential and failure of love govern the second half, though Nobuko, Varda and Leontine each offer a portrait of what might happen if the artist herself internalizes the detritus or ruin—in Varda's case to literally make art out of that ruin, the scraps left behind.

In the final three episodes, the scene shifts abruptly to New York where Renate has gone to an exhibit of her paintings. Two jarring things happen in the closing pages of *Collages*. First, the sunny and hopeful western landscape is replaced by the gritty and harsh New York. This atmospheric shift is made doubly harsh by the recounting of the story of Lisa, a once successful artist in Mexico who has allowed herself to be imprisoned in a terrible marriage with a man who doesn't understand her, a man who "awakened her from her dream of

Acapulco with a cigar flavored kiss from the ashcan painting period of her childhood."

And secondly, after providing the McGuffin for the closing episode taking place in New York, Renate more or less disappears as a protagonist from the book. As the closing of *Ladders to Fire* was taken away from Lillian and given to Sabina and Djuna, as the narrator of *House of Incest* becomes a spectator in the closing scene of that book, so too is the closing of *Collages* given to the new character of Doctor Mann, who has come to New York from Israel to search for the elusive writer Judith Sands.

Dr. Mann feels that he is the character in Sands' book and is obsessed with meeting her face to face. But before you read these episodes as weird non-sequitur, consider that Dr. Mann himself is another facet of Renate. Nin met the painter Renate Druks in California and used her portrait, along with those of Varda, of Josephine Premice (the basis for Leontine), and of others she knew like Lesley Branch, as materials in constructing this novel, just like one of Varda's collages.

Rather than doing the deep internal analysis that Nin's earlier characters do, these characters seem content with telling their own stories and allowing the reader to construct meaning on her own.

And so the drama of Doctor Mann (who seems much like the character of Matthew O'Connor from Djuna Barnes' book *Nightwood*) and Judith Sands (a caricature-portrait of the elusive Barnes) can be read also as an encounter between Renate Druks the real woman and Anaïs Nin as well as an expression of Nin's ongoing disappointment that the real Barnes did not want to meet her.

Similarly, Tinguely's machine that destroys itself that appears at the exhibit that Mann, Sands and Renate attend at the end of the novel can be seen as a figure for the book. It is significant that as the machine (the novel?) destroys itself, Renate rescues the strip with the artists' names and the group of friends plans to repair to a bar to read the names to one another. *Collages* is itself a 'continuous novel.' It eddies around itself, proving the endlessly generative possibilities of art.

Hans, the painter from the story "The Eye's Journey" in *Under a Glass Bell*, knows the lesson. He lives in his mind, "at the bottom of the sea cluttered with objects from shipwrecks." Using these materials in his paintings, he always paints a human eye in the corner of each one: "the secret door of his escape into the deep regions unknown."

Hans, unfortunately, cannot function as well in daily society. He hasn't paid rent in a year, and he lives in fear of being arrested or being served poisoned soup by the concierge; he is sure the two men who have come to see him are there to steal his paintings and kill him.

The ability of the artist to have a vision at all is at stake in "The Eye's Journey." An artist who is so fixated on the internal that he does not see the world around him for how it truly exists is likened, for his limited vision, to a man with a glass eye. But the artists in *Collages* know well how to connect the internal with the external. The novel itself, when seen alongside the earliest stories Nin wrote (now published as *Waste of Timelessness*), shows a sophisticated architecture of form, from those stories through *House of Incest* and the more polished stories of *Under a Glass Bell* and both versions of *Winter of Artifice*. One could see all these books being published in a single volume to conclude with *Ladders to Fire,* and the last four novels of *Cities of the Interior* joining *Collages* in a second full volume. Then the full range of Nin's achievements as a fiction writer could be more clearly seen.

Diane Richard-Allerdyce also saw *Collages* as precisely that investigation between Nin's modernist approach to fiction and what would later follow: "*Collages* participates in the questioning of artistic categories and genre boundaries typical of Postmodern theory, even as Nin remained thoroughly Modern in her emphasis on structure as an organizing element in art."[8] Nin herself was candid about the connection. In *Novel of the Future*, she writes, "By 1966 it was the experience of the novelist which helped me edit the diary. It was the fiction writer who knew when the tempo lagged, when details were trivial, when a description was a repetition."[9]

Finally, at the end (and *Collages* does *feel* like an ending), Nin returns back to her original sources, life itself—in the novel's case, Renate's life, but finally Nin's own as depicted in the *Diary*—but always fiction and diary have their sources in one another. It is a two-way street, as circular and multidirectional as the rivers of music Djuna traverses in her mind.

---

8. Diane Richard-Allerdyce, *Anaïs Nin and the Remaking of the Self: Gender, Modernism and Narrative Identity,* (DeKalb: Northern Illinois Press, 1998), 139.
9. Nin, *Novel of the Future*, 124.

Instruction Painting:
A Blueprint for an Installation

A large room should be used, with a double-sided screen dropped in the middle, dividing it in two. Viewers/audients can proceed clockwise to view the exhibit in order, or can move among them, seeing them in any order.

On the side of the screen facing the entrance, Jean Varda's *Women Reconstructing the World* is displayed. The other side of the screen runs the film *Anaïs Nin Observed* by Robert Snyder.

Station #1:

"Vienna was a city of statues."
Painting, oil. 12" wide by 36."
A view of the cityscape through a window; window frame barely seen. City seen by moonlight, grey, charcoal and black, the sides of the buildings and the statues illuminated in one side by the silvery-yellow moonlight, much brighter than it would ordinarily be, made brighter by the gaze of the viewer as well. Human statues in the front. They can be observed, touched, but not manipulated.

Black silhouettes of birds fly along the white wall of the gallery to the next station. In between each station, the birds get subtly greyer and lighter until they are white and then they darken again to finish as black once more, by the final station.

Station #2:

"When Bruce came to Vienna."
Installation.
A bed to lie in, a door just beyond, open to the wall, a road stretching out in the dark painted on the wall. Two figures under the tree. One must unlock the door to look through and then walk through the door to continue.

Station #3:

"Renate moved to Malibu, California."
Sculpture.
A wooden box mounted on the wall. One must take the hanging key and unlock it. Inside the box a dove carved out of paper-thin wood. When one opens the door of the box one can hear soft sounds of the beach—the ocean, the gulls, the horns of boats.

Station #4:

"Behind Renate's house lay the mountain."
Painting, acrylic: 36" by 48".
Bruce as Pan. On a small shelf before the painting, Chinese puzzle boxes for the viewer to open. Inside the boxes, rolled up, text from *Collages,* Bruce's story: "When I first met Ken I was seventeen..." etc. Other boxes may contain other parts of the novel or Bruce's other stories may be imagined, or

text harvested from viewer responses to the exhibit can be included.

Station #5:

"Renate gathered together all the linen of the house..."
Mixed media.
Soiled sheets mounted on stretchers. Should be soiled by the artist with bodily fluids of any kind; ideally involving other participants. All parties should be designated as creators of the piece in accompanying signage.

Station #6:

"In the small towns of California..."
Mixed media.
Painting on loan: "Raven" by Renate Druks. Frame decorated with black raven feathers. Text from this chapter of collages written on ticker tape to unspool and tear off and take away.

Station #7:

"While driving along the Pacific Palisades..."
Mixed media.
A triptych of paintings, oil. First and third panels, 18" by 36". Second panel, 36" by 36". First panel: A portrait of an old man as described in the text. Second panel: A seascape of the underside of the pier in Santa Cruz, California, the seals and sea lions, resting above the water. Third Panel: Portrait of the old man diving beneath the waves, transforming to a seal. Soundtrack: the sounds and calls of the seals and sea lions.

Station #8:

"When Renate did not sell enough paintings..."
Mixed media.
Fragment of a table mounted from the wall, with plate, silverware and glass half-filled with wine. *Trompe-lœil* of the Paradise Inn, painted beyond the table. Headphones with ambient sounds and Leontine singing.

Station #9:

"Henri the chef was the adopted son of the famous Escoffier."
Performance.
If a viewer actually seats himself at the table and lifts the silverware and/or takes a drink of the wine, a waiter will appear and serve that person a crêpe Suzette.

Station #10:

"Varda lived on a converted ferry boat..."
Learning station.
A video of Varda plays. Varda's art is displayed. A book on Varda is there to peruse.

Station #11:

"When Renate and Varda met..."
Interactive exhibit.
Swathes of fabric are available, as well as other materials, beads, shells, etc. Scissors, thread, glue and glue-gun available to create a collaborative collage, hung from the wall and begun by the installers of the exhibit. A box should be provided for visitors who wish to cut and leave a swatch of fabric from their own clothing.

Station #12:

"Bruce and Renate entered a dimly-lit café..."
Sound installation.
Ear-phones over which play a cacophony of Nina. An actress should recite Nina's dialogue and then these should be mixed and overlapped in a composition of sound.

Station #13:

"Nobuko was small and dainty."
Mixed media installation.
Series of mixed media canvases, each 16" by 16". First: bright yellow silk with black velvet obi. Second: dove grey silk with bright orange obi painted across it. Third: Purple jacaranda silk with gold obi. A small box with purple tissue paper letter, orange tissue paper letter, and several blank sheets of pearl grey paper with a pen. The viewer is invited to write a letter and send, via box with a mail-slot.

Station #14:

"The French consulate..."
Reading station.
Lesley Branch's book. Also a simulacrum of the consul's wife's materials, her notes and the "precious notes, letters, sketches" as well as maps and manuscripts of the war hero. These can be charred as if rescued from the burning plane. Above, mounted on the wall, an unfinished sampler reading, "Nothing is ever finished."

Station #15:

"Colonel Tishnar came..."

Installation.
Copies of the pearl-grey letters from Station #13 are hung from the wall and ceiling in strings of various length so they can be perused. When seen from a distance, they should take a shape of a bird in flight or other sculptural image in space.

Station #16:

"Renate grew tired of painting portraits..."
Guest-book.
Bound books are available for the participants to write their impressions of the exhibit. One book should be divided into sections according to each station. The other book is blank and open for holistic impressions.

Station #17:

"Renate and Lisa had met in Acapulco..."
Mixed media. Painting: 48" by 48".
A view through Lisa's apartment window. Outside, a cold New York City streetscape crossed by "the stripes of dusty sunlight falling through the rails of the Third Avenue Elevated trains." At the edges of the frame the interior of the apartment is seen—bright colors, Mexican textiles and objects, in contrast to the view through the window. Soundtrack: earphones playing Mexican music.

Station #18:

"The bell rang. It was Doctor Mann..."
Item on loan: "Machine That Destroys Itself," Jean Tinguely.
Machine can played by pressing a button or turning a crank.

Station #19:

"The crowd dispersed."
As many different copies of *Collages*, in various editions, as can be collected. A table or other small reading station can be provided. A call for book objects or art-books based on the text of *Collages* should be issued in advance of the exhibit, and these objects included in Station #19. Copies of the call for works should be included in Station #19 and any further submissions should also be included as they are received.

Optional soundtrack for Station #19: A live performer singing Renate's sailing song.

Il était un petit navire/ Qui n'avait ja-ja-jamais navigué

The music is heard in different parts of the room and intermittently fades away.

He was a little sailor boy/ who ne-e-e-ver sailed before...

Boats

When writer Meena Alexander was asked at a reading what kind of house she would live in, if she could choose any that she wanted—she chose instead a boat. "It would have to float," she said, "though I would settle for a tent...tethered to a cloud. A floating tent. A tent for a poet who finds it hard to be securely in place."[1]

Boats recur throughout Nin's work: boats moored at the quays of the Seine, boats cut loose of their mooring and floating down the river, boats lost in dreams, pulled from the sea and used as a garden shed. Boats dragged through the city. Boats taking on water. Boats sinking, boats being bailed out.

The voyages, both psychic and physical, that these boats bear their passengers through are just as varied.

Like Alexander, the narrator of Nin's story "Waste of Timelessness" chooses a boat over a house. She is on her way to a weekend party being given for the writer Alain Roussel. Accompanied by talkative friends with whom she does not

---

1. Meena Alexander, *Poetics of Dislocation,* (Ann Arbor: University of Michigan Press, 2009), ix.

connect and who complain about the stormy weather, she imagines the house blowing away in a strong wind and then the writer himself walking along the road, inviting her to instead "spend the weekend on that old fishing boat on the beach."[2]

The boat represents a refuge away from the closed, domestic life—the one that wants the wisteria to grow only a certain way over the doorframe, that complains about the beautiful rain.

There, in the garden of the house, she sees an old Norman fishing boat. It had been converted into a garden shed, though once they put a bed inside for a little boy guest. Once she knows of the existence of the boat, the narrator is able to suffer through the inane dinner conversation much more easily. Like Alexander's floating tent, she knows it is out there, connected to her by invisible threads: "the very old boat which had traveled far, now sunk in a quiet dark garden."[3]

That night, when she leaves the house in her nightgown, they are shocked. They had not thought she truly meant to sleep there, and though they try to stop her she runs down the path and unfastens the mildewed rope tying it to a tree, throwing it off into the darkness. "And now I am gone," she says.

She dreams in the night of *really* leaving: "Certainly on this boat I could drift away from this world down some strange wise river into strange wise places..." And then the story takes a turn into magical realism of a sort: "In the morning, the boat was no longer in the garden. Her husband took the 2:25 train home to talk this problem over with his partner."[4]

She drifts through the night on the boat. She sees plenty of

---

2. Nin, *Waste of Timelessness* (n.p.: Magic Circle Press, 1977), 1.
3. Ibid., 3
4. Ibid., 4.

potential harbors but they all seem to be "ordinary-looking places."

Finally, she even sees Roussel, the famous writer. But since he is already mobbed by worshippers, she pushes on.

Eventually, she sees her husband, who begs her to come home for a dinner party that evening. "That is not a destination," she says, and continues.

She dreamt of using the boat to escape, but now adrift she can find nothing worth escaping to. Even when she sees other boats, the people in them are not using them for transformative purposes but just for "rest from ordinary living."

When she sees Roussel again, she realizes she has inadvertently traveled a circle. He accuses her of running away from life. Her old hosts need their garden tools, he admonishes her.

She drifts on, finally wishing to be home, and wakes up in the garden. Without her presence or awareness, twenty years have passed. "I have been wasting a lot of time," she admits.[5]

A narrator again falls asleep on a boat and undergoes transformation in the story "Houseboat," from *Under a Glass Bell*.

The narrator wants to live on the water because its current is pure and even, not like the current of life in the streets of the city, "made of dissonant pieces colliding rustily, driven by hunger and desire."[6]

Even the homeless people who live on the quays appeal to

---

5. Ibid., 6
6. Nin, *Under a Glass Bell,* (Athens: Swallow Press), 1948, 11.

her, having "abandoned time, possessions, labor, slavery."

In her houseboat, she feels she has "a life in the infinite," separated from the city and geography; she feels a kinship with the Unknown Woman of the Seine, who had drowned herself in the river some years earlier and who was so beautiful the police had taken a cast of her face.

She waits in the dark for her phantom lover, and while she sleeps the boat somehow moves. A woman is drowning outside; her screams awaken the narrator, who rushes outside to watch the woman rescued by the "shipwrecked mariners" who live on the quay.

A child sits further on, crying. Like Mathilda, the woman on the quays in *Children of the Albatross,* he has been abandoned by his mother, who told him to wait.

She is on a mythical journey now. Each night she sleeps and the boat is in a different place with different metaphysical dangers, and even, once, in a calm place of light. But even there, as she is racing toward the festival, she discovers men with scythes cutting the algae plants in the water.

When she wakes from this last dream, a dream of the island of joy that still is unfulfilling, reality awaits: the King of England is coming to Paris for a visit and all the boats are ordered to sail up the Seine and out of the city to an old boatyard.

In this way, the political and material realities of the day trump the days of rootlessness and loose living, of floating on the surface of the river and dreaming of endlessness each evening. The king leaves, but they are not permitted to return and "so passed the barge into exile."

If boats stand for a certain freedom of living, they can also be places of danger and insularity. For Djuna in *Four-Chambered*

Heart, the houseboat on which she lives and conducts her affair with Rango is a symbol of imprisonment and stasis. For both Lillian in *Solar Barque* and Renate in *Collages,* the dream of a boat becomes a chance—for Lillian to leave everyone behind her and follow her own destiny for once, and for Renate a last chance to save a relationship that feels doomed.

When Djuna and Rango leave the café after their first meeting they walk "instinctively toward the river," for Djuna a symbol of freedom from her previous life. She is attracted to Rango's background, his rootlessness, but when they arrive at his house, she can "not bear yet to see how he had been captured, tamed, caged, by what circumstances, by whom."[7]

Djuna and Rango decide they need a boat in order to live freely of Djuna's responsibility to her ill father and Rango's responsibility to his ill wife, Zora. They search and though they do not like the fact that all the boats resemble houses— "Why bring to a barge the same trimmings as those of a house? They are not made for the river, these people, not for voyages."—they find one that had once been used by a troupe of actors to travel across the country.

There, in the depths of the boat, Djuna worries that Rango, from the mountains, will be out of his element floating on water. He kisses her so passionately the lantern is knocked over and flames break out, but the oil is quickly absorbed by the thick, dry floor and the fire goes out. Djuna is delighted: "She watched it without fear… she had always wanted to live near danger."[8]

Though they find their rootless existence possible without the crushing and confining influences of land-locked life, they are unable to protect themselves from its influences. Their life on the boat is not secure—they do not have a padlock, and

---

7. Nin, *Cities*, 243.
8. Ibid, 250.

though Rango promises to secure one, he does not, and their belongings are always missing.

It bothers Djuna but not Rango, who even when land-locked was always rootless, his possessions "scattered all over the world, in rooming house cellars where they were kept as hostages for unpaid rent." She images all the little flames from the spilled lantern burning within him all "except the wise one of the holy ghost."

This rootlessness of living on the boat, floating on the river, rising and falling with the tides and Rango's temper is such a contrast to the deep-rootedness of Djuna's house, the one she chose because it had no cellar, because it rested directly on the earth.

They are able to continue their imprisoned love only because they keep it on the boat as their sanctuary. They are unable to withstand the pressures of the outside world at all. First, Rango wants Djuna to meet his hypochondriac wife, Zora, who is aware of their affair. Then Djuna takes Rango and Zora to the ocean shore, so Zora can convalesce. Finally, Rango asks that Djuna allow his political group to use the boat as a meeting place.

Each of these external influences deals blows to the relationship.

Djuna has a hard time allowing politics to enter their refuge: "The only remedy is to begin a world of two; in two there is hope of perfection, and that in turn may spread to all." Rango is impatient: "I'm going to give you books to read, to study."[9] After asking Djuna to burn her books of literature, poetry, philosophy, Rango now wants to indoctrinate Djuna with his kind of knowledge, knowledge for the betterment of

---

9. Ibid, 337.

society; but for Djuna, like Nin, societal change must begin with knowledge of the self.

At any rate, the political meeting falls apart because of security issues. Rather than going back to their isolated existence, though, Djuna takes Rango's cue: the barge becomes a meeting place for all of her bohemian and artistic friends. Their conflict between responsibility to personal need and political abstraction drives them apart.

The boat is also the scene for their final drama—Zora appears one night and attacks Djuna with a hatpin. Ironically, she blames Djuna for Rango's political involvement. When Rango is unable to act, Djuna experiences her final disillusionment at his inertia.

While they live on the boat, it is moored to the pier; they are going nowhere.

After Rango sleeps, Djuna wanders the empty front cabin with its "portholes like the windows of a prison," and leans over to pull up the "old and half-rotted" plants in order to allow "the deluge to sink this Noah's Ark sailing nowhere."[10]

The reality of the boat becomes the symbol of Djuna's failure.

When Lillian leaves her husband and life in Paris, it is because of a recurrent dream "of a ship that could not reach the water, that sailed laboriously, pushed by her with great effort, through city streets."[11]

In a stunning example of the intentional interior transference between characters, the astute reader will remember this is actually *Djuna's* dream, one she recounts to Lillian at the beginning of *Ladders to Fire*.[12]

---

10. Ibid, 352.
11. Ibid, 465.
12. Ibid, 25.

After leaving her family, Lillian arrives in Mexico to play at The Black Pearl, a jazz club, and finds there a reality of golden life, unlike the previous metaphorical gold recounted earlier in Djuna's dreams in both *Ladders* and *Children of the Albatross*.

In a sense, Lillian at the beginning of her own quest starts actualizing in concrete reality what had previously only been Djuna's abstractions.

Wanting to keep the mythical city for herself, free of the tourists that swarmed around it, she christens it 'Golconda,' but she can't help but think of the complicated history of the city in terms of all the ships and boats that have visited it—the Japanese shipwreck, the slave ships from Africa, the Spanish galley that was wrecked and "scattered across the beach baptism dresses which the women…had adopted as headgear." Later, to get away from the tourist trap of the city, her new friend Doctor Hernandez takes her in a hand-carved canoe, painted a bright blue that had faded to "the smoky blue of Mayan murals, a blue which man could not create, only time."[13]

It is the same blue that, later in the story, colors a prison cell, connecting the liberation possible in the figure of the boat with the danger involved—danger Djuna is aware of, danger that the woman visiting the house of the writer has also confronted.

As the boat glides through the jungle vegetation, Lillian remembers her dream. Sometimes the boat is a huge multi-decked galley, other times it is small, but always "caught in a waterless place." She feels suddenly the dream has ended, that in Golconda "she had attained a flowing life, a flowing journey."

---

13. Ibid, 481.

She remembers the story she heard of the Egyptian pharaoh and their solar barques: "There were always two: one buried in limestone and unable to float on the waterless routes of anxiety, the other flowing continuously with life. The static one made the voyage of memories, and the floating one proceeded into endless discoveries."[14]

Not all of the transformations or journeys in Nin's work are welcome. In *Seduction of the Minotaur,* not until he is on the deck of the ship is the character Fred able to realize he wants to stay in Mexico. While at the yacht party, Dr. Hernandez experiences a personality transformation that indirectly leads him into danger. Later, when Lillian takes a night journey on a bus to visit another friend in Mexico, she realizes with distress, "She had been unable to live for three months a new life, in a new city, without being caught by an umbilical cord and brought back to the figure of her father."[15]

Later, in *Collages,* in an effort to save their relationship, feeling they cannot live their Mexico life in California, Renate and Bruce buy a little sailboat in Holland and decide to sail while Bruce writes his novel and Renate paints.

The duties on board prove too onerous, and so they decide to furl the sails and travel by motor. When the motor stalls, they find themselves in the middle of a river, becalmed. Finally, Bruce decides they need more space to move around in and has the boat taken to drydock, where they load it onto a train and travel to the Mediterranean.

Nin revisits her earlier scene of a boat sinking, but unlike the psychological drama of Djuna pulling up planks to sink the boat, here the scene is played for laughs: the caulking has melted on the long rail voyage south and the boat begins sinking. Unlike Rango, the indolent Bruce will not rouse

---

14. Ibid, 483.
15. Ibid, 531.

himself at Renate's urging and the boat sinks. Unlike Djuna, Renate seems unbothered by the tragedy and while Bruce jumps out to swim and pull the swiftly sinking vessel back to dry-dock, she pumps and sings an old French sailing song. "From now on," she tells Bruce gaily, "our travels will have to be inner voyages."[16]

Lillian, traveling home finally, in the coda section added to *Solar Barque* to make *Seduction of the Minotaur*, finds her real wholeness not in Sabina's concept of fractured selves, each which grows at its own speed and needs to fuse with the others, nor in Djuna's notion of the heart with four chambers, each separate and with its own capabilities; rather, she swims at last in the waters, no longer ensconced in the boat. She feels the water on her skin, surrenders her notions of fixity and rigidity, and begins to feel all things that flow into and out of one another.

She compares this feelings to the sounds of *musique concrète*, "the echo in vast space which corresponds to new dimensions in science, the echo which was never heard in classical music."[17] Her feelings mirror, in some ways, those of Djuna's as she lies by the torn up planks, waiting for her boat to sink: "Below the level of identity lay an ocean…Beneath the cities of interior flowed many rivers carrying a multitude of images…All the women she had been spread their hair in a halo on the surface of the river, extending their multiple arms like the idols of India…"[18] One is reminded here of the drowned doll, the Unknown Woman of the Seine, the armless dancer, Mathilda waiting by the pier, all the other women Nin has invoked throughout her fiction.

In this watery vision, Djuna sees herself as many women and

---

16. Nin, *Collages* (Athens: Swallow Press. 1964), 26.
17. Nin, *Cities*, 588.
18. Ibid, 352.

realizes, like Lillian in Mexico, "fixation is death…the voyage can continue until tomorrow…she would learn from Sabina how to make love laughing, and from Stella how to die only for a little while and be reborn."[19]

What brings her back to consciousness, why she decides to save the boat, is that the boat was not just built for her individual love with Rango, which has failed, but for the idea of love. She wakes Rango. They plug the leak.

Walking along the quays that morning, one of the fishermen pulls from the water a doll, which had fallen into the river, washed clear of its features, like Djuna becoming one and every woman.

---

19. Ibid, 353-4.

The Voice

When Zora lunges at Djuna out of the dark, hatpin in her hands, Djuna is able to fight her off by analyzing her. It's not meant to be comic. And what's breathtaking is that by that point in *Cities of the Interior,* it doesn't *feel* comic. Djuna has already failed at analyzing herself and knowing herself in the party scene at the end of *Ladders to Fire.* Similarly, she turns away from the external world and her disappointment at losing Paul in the climax of *Children of the Albatross.*

Those failures at love are what set her up for the self-punishing relationship she put herself through throughout *Four-Chambered Heart.* What's funny, if anything, about her speech to Zora, is that Djuna could know others so well and still be so stuck in her relationship with Rango.

Of course, her freeing of Zora via on-the-spot analysis and Rango's subsequent inability to grow at all from the experience is what precipitates her decision to sink the boat.

Though Nin herself used to say that of her women only Lillian achieved liberation, Djuna does actually free herself at the end of this book, as evidenced by the surfacing of the doll without features. Though unable to save herself, Djuna goes on to provide the intellectual impetus for salvation to both Sabina and Lillian in the two later novels.

How is one saved? Lillian is saved by experience, only by living through something. Sabina must be saved by another. Djuna saves by the intellect, by understanding; with it she is able to help others along their paths, but her own liberation comes only when she is able to face the fire within herself.

The counterpoint of intellect and experience between Djuna and Lillian is duplicated by characters in the novels who exist outside the framework of the plot, nameless male characters known only by their attributes: the Lie Detector, the Voice, the Chess Player and even, though briefly, the research scientist in *Children of the Albatross*.

These characters fulfill 'analyst' roles, interacting with the protagonist characters and helping them to see their own courses of action. Djuna's liberation is that by the end of the *Cities of the Interior* cycle she has learned how to assume this role, how to help Lillian and Sabina, though whether she has been able to help herself is not shown. The Lie Detector is supplanted by Djuna at the conclusion of *Spy in the House of Love;* by *Seduction of the Minotaur,* this archetypal nameless character is missing completely; perhaps not coincidentally, it is the first novel written "without any dependence on the diary."[1]

In *Seduction of the Minotaur,* the character of the external analyst, Dr. Hernandez, is no longer anonymous and is a fully realized character with desires and motivations of his own. Lillian thinks to herself at the beginning of the novel about his resemblance to the Lie Detector, and later at the yacht party he takes on aspects of the Chess Player, manipulating

---

1. Nin, *Novel of the Future,* 140.

the situation and the people around him. By *Collages*, Nin has moved past the question of the individual and into the larger canvas based on multiplicity (not just of the self) and interrelationships.

Nin wants the dreams and inner life of her characters to *be* the plot. If some critics have suggested that people don't *really* talk like this, Nin suggests: but maybe they *should*.

In "Realism and Reality," she suggests "with all the evasions of the essential inner drama practiced by the so-called realistic novel…we are actually being constantly cheated of reality and experience."[2]

She wants to leave out the furnishings of Stella's apartment, the "upholstery" as she calls it, in order to, in almost synesthetic fashion, depict the inner movements and subterranean moods. "The richest source of creation is feeling," she says. "The medium of a writer is not ink and paper but his body: the sensitivity of his eyes, ears and heart."[3]

That is perhaps why the division between the external authority of a character who sees from the outside diminishes over the course of the books—from the extreme remove of The Voice, to the Chess Player who actually attends the party though he remains apart from the other guests, to the Lie Detector, who stalks Sabina, following her from one place to another and actually speaks with her twice, once at the novel's beginning and once at its end. Finally, you have Lillian and Dr. Hernandez, whom she says reminds her of the Lie Detector, who have a fully functional and interactive relationship.

Nin goes on to explain that "the collective neurosis" brought on by our "current social structure" of alienation and isolation "can be explored and dealt with only under conditions of tremendously

---

2. Nin, *Mystic of Sex,* 26.
3. Ibid., 31.

high atmospheric pressures, temperatures and speed, as well as in terms of new time-space dimensions for which the old containers represented by the traditional forms and conventions of the novel are completely inadequate and inappropriate."[4]

The distraught Djuna agrees the burn her books.

A Spy in the House of Love is episodic and fragmented because character reveals itself most clearly and cleanly in "moments of emotional crisis"[5]; these are the moments when "the real self rises to the surface." It is a novel, literally, on fire.

Children of the Albatross, obsessed with air and Djuna's airy nature, has thus the structure of the ballet with its leaps and jumps,[6] while *Four-Chambered Heart,* according to Nin, "has the structure of a river."[7]

Science and scientific fact has, through the scientist, an illustrative impact in *Children of the Albatross*. It is a poetic leap from her conversation with Michael and Donald and her feelings of alienation to the scientist's brief lecture on the reasons birds can fly, the hollowness of their bones. It is followed immediately by the entrance of Paul, bird-as-man, and Djuna's attempt to "fly" with him, taking "leaps into the air."

The Lie Detector has a stranger and more exciting role. Though external, he is a version of Sabina's conscience. Being unable to face her own deeds, she reaches out blindly to anyone she can find. She does not anticipate the man actually being interested and following her, watching her, taking notes.

Her fear that he will arrest her, it holds in it a kernel of *wanting*

---

4. Ibid., 34.
5. Ibid., 37.
6. Nin, *Novel of the Future*, 80.
7. Ibid., 83.

to be arrested, wanting to be caught and made to account for her actions.

He is the one who is able to make her see that everyone has the fragmented nature that until then she had only been seeing in herself: "Could you go out now and find the other faces of Alan, which you never struggled to see or accept? Would you find the other face of Mambo...would you struggle to find the other face of Philip?"

"I AM THE OTHER FACE OF YOU," the narrator of *House of Incest* declares to Sabina in her first appearance in that book. "YOU ARE THE WOMAN I AM." Whereas in *House of Incest*, this transference is seen as flawed, by *Spy in the House of Love*, Nin implies that a recognition of the other's true nature via a similar empathy is indeed possible.

When, in the end, Sabina weeps as Djuna plays music, the Lie Detector, perhaps callously, still wants her to face up to her actions—to see that the emotional response to the music is still only a symptom of her self-destruction and is not the same as intellectually understanding her circumstance.

The Chess Player is not emotionally invested in the people he is manipulating, and no one really knows his motivation, "for he was content with the displacements and did not share in the developments." Like Nin leaning against the wall in the Deren film, after he guided a group together he would retreat and watch from a distance.

Djuna, of course, with her "smiling masks" and "blurred absences" is on to him from the start, but allows herself to be paired up with an Irish architect who begins designing a perfect house, "drawing a blueprint on her dress."

The Chess Player loses a piece when he guides Faustin to Sabina, but she, too full already, turns her "camellia face" away.

As the Chess Player watches the various motions and interactions at the party—between Rango and Djuna, Jay and Hans the dutch painter, Stella—he sees Sabina taking her cape and making for the balcony. "She was making a gradual escape," he knew. "He could not allow this to go on, at a Party everyone should pursue nothing but his individual drama."

Like at Mrs. Dalloway's party, Nin's narrative awareness shifts into Sabina and follows her out onto the balcony, where she worries about "the broken compass which inhabited her and whose wild fluctuations she had always obeyed."

Sabina, unlike the others at the party, is manipulated from the inside. She is her own wild chess player and does not submit to the conversation with Faustin; rather, she finds herself alone on the balcony.

But inside the party, the Chess Player does not give up his game. Distracted by Stella and by dispersing of the party, he misses Lillian, "alone on a square," berating herself for being too late, too coarse, unsure of herself. All the Chess Player can notice is the external not the internal.

While Lillian confesses in her inner voice her secret fear of going to play at a concert where "the piano had no notes, it was a lake, and I tried to play on the water and no sound came," all the Chess Player saw is "a woman crumpling down on a couch as if her inner frame had collapsed." He sees "her drunkenness and took no note of the internal suicide."[8]

What he doesn't realize at all is that her "inner frame" *has* collapsed—not her skeleton, but her self-vision and self-understanding. "All these people have accomplished something and I have not...I hate the way my hair gets wild... Why do I rush and speak before thinking?" Lillian continues berating herself.

---

8. Nin, *Cities*, 124.

He manipulates people, but has no understanding of their inner emotional lives. And it is only intuitive Djuna that catches a glimpse of this, "where a blighted love had made its first incision and the blood had turned to tree sap to become wood."[9]

A character called the Voice appears in one of Nin's earliest fictions, as the analyst who treats Djuna, Mischa, Lilith and Lillian in *Winter of Artifice.*

He is introduced as a removed character, separate, like the Chess Player, interfacing with his patients, but not becoming emotionally drawn to them, "the little man no one ever saw."

He must, though, enter into their secrets—which Lilith feels, panicking, as an "invasion." Of course, ultimately, she sublimates her feelings of gratitude to him, thinking she is falling in love with him. The Voice is having none of it: "Even when they love me, it is a love that is not addressed to me. I remain anonymous."

"I feel the real you behind the analyst," Lilith insists. "I am only a symbol," he counters.[10]

What happens in this conversation in the original version of this story, which appeared in the 1939 book *The Winter of Artifice*—a 'deleted scene' if you will—is racier. Lilith exposes her breasts to the Voice in an effort to seduce him. He is tempted but demurs, clinging to his argument.[11]

Later, in a session with Djuna, he does all the talking, confessing that if Lilith truly loved him for himself, not for the symbol, that he would give up his work to be with her.

---

9. Ibid., 126.
10. Nin, *Winter of Artifice,* (Athens: Swallow Press, 1946), 110.
11. Nin, *The Winter of Artifice: a facsimile,* 239.

Unfortunately, he tells her, "we are all alike, and my patients desperately do not want me to be like them."[12]

Djuna empathizes with the position of the man, "sitting and listening all day, pinned to his confessions, disguised by the anonymity of vision, and desiring to play an active, personal role in these scenes perpetually unfolding before him."[13]

Strange to see such a removed character, so sketched in outline, struggling to insist on himself, that his desires also be a part of the story.

Lilith confesses her desires to Djuna: "I feel he is a soul detective, and that day he captures me, I will love him."[14] Djuna tries to help Lilith see see that her love for the Voice is a "mirage." "Why don't I find a man who makes me feel what I feel with you?" Lilith muses plaintively as they lie together in the dark, entangled in each other's arms.

Nin, seemingly still unable to confront the fullness of lesbian sexuality, turns it back to her old concept of "incest," of loving the self in the other. Djuna says, "But none of this is love, Lilith. We are the same woman. There is always the moment when all the outlines, the differences between women disappear and we enter a world where all feelings, yours and mine, seem to issue from the same source."

When Lilith confronts the Voice again, he turns his back on his own desires and helps her to see "It was a father she was looking for, not a lover." This realization, far from preventing them pursuing a relationship, is what allows them to do so.

As they come to know each other better, she begins asking

---

12. Nin, *Winter of Artifice,* 113.
13. Ibid., 114.
14. Ibid., 117.

him questions about his childhood; he weeps, because he is now in the position of being listened to.

While they get to know each other more and more, he begins "deciphering each incident" in her life. This does not help her to know herself better, but rather "she began to feel the illusory quality" of all interpretation.

She realizes her own feelings are a better map than all the intellectual analysis—he remains to her, in the end, "nothing but A VOICE."[15]

The original *Winter of Artifice* has an even more expanded version of the relationship between Lilith and the Voice. After Lilith and Djuna's conversation, Lilith wants Djuna to attend Mischa's concert with her, but Djuna has gotten some opium and plans to use it to dream. Lilith and The Voice attend Mischa's concert together instead, and later go to the seashore together. Their relationship unfolds over several pages that are juxtaposed with Djuna's extended dream.

It is at the shore that Lilith realizes that The Voice "with his pulpy hat in his hand, entangled in his valises" does not embody her desire after all, but instead "remained nothing but the Voice."[16]

Nin perhaps suppressed this extension of the story because it paralleled too closely her own romantic and sexual relationship with her analyst Otto Rank, upon whom the character of The Voice is based. In the revised *Winter of Artifice,* the relationship between Lilith and The Voice remains platonic and the story ends in Djuna's dream.

Separations diminish between these external, Greek Chorus-

---

15. Ibid., 126.
16. Nin, *The Winter of Artifice: a facsimile,* 289.

like characters and the people around them. The Lie Detector receives Sabina's late night phone call and, like the Voice, is not content to remain in the abstract.

Djuna is able to find her own freedom, eventually, because she is able to really see and understand herself.

In the new version of *The Winter of Artifice,* the novel does not end with Lilith's failure to love the Voice, but rather with Djuna deep inside her dream. As Stella ascended the spiral staircase, retreating farther and farther within herself at the beginning of *Winter of Artifice,* her dream Djuna enters a dream-like stage and ascends a spiral tower.

She dreams for the first time of the boat that "was passing through the city unable to find the ocean that transmitted its life voyages." Deep within her dream in this early book, situated between *House of Incest* and *Children of the Albatross,* Djuna searches for the elusive window, the "window of a house I had lived in, I could not remember when."[17]

She realizes the marriage between the internal and the external. Unlike Stella, or perhaps on behalf of Stella, in her dream Djuna is able to understand "the life on the stage, the life of the legend dovetailed with the daylight, and out of this marriage sparked the great birds of divinity, the eternal moments."

---

17. Nin, *Winter of Artifice,* 129.

Coda

Anaïs Nin made a space in the novel between poetry and prose.

We had to wait to see her. Text reveals itself anew. Each veil drops, but it is the clothing draped on the bedroom floor that tells the story of the bodies in love.

Her brother Joaquin wrote about her: "She was a woman with one hundred faces and perhaps needs one hundred people to write her biography."

Routes between the diary and the novels exhaustively mapped.

Carla Harryman: "If we are referring to her diaries, Nin wrote in much closer proximity to actual experience than I, if actual experience is taken to be what happens. If we are referring to her novels, then, instead, the writing is a dream or dream state being enacted on the page. The diary is produced by referring to an event proximate to Nin's *act* of writing, whereas the dream of the novel *is* the writing."[1]

---

1. Harryman, Carla. *Adorno's Noise* (n.p.: Essay Press, 2008), 16.

Novel as ritual, as shadow theater.

Novel as a river that flows from one book to the next. No continuing plot but the lives of characters.

Nin from *Novel of the Future:* "I was asked why I used the same characters over a long period. The diary taught me the interest there in watching development and growth."[2]

The diaries are a different kind of novel, each chosen, selected, excerpted; each set feels different. *The Diary of Anaïs Nin, Volumes 1-6,* selected and edited and reworked and revised by Nin herself, has the closest feel to a constructed novel. Beginning with *Diary 7* and through the *Early Diaries* and now the "Unexpurgated" *Diaries,* one senses different textures and tones according the hands of the editors—first Gunther Stuhlmann, then Rupert Pole, now Paul Herron.

Nin herself talks of retiring as the "main character" of the *Diary,* much like Lillian and Renate each "retire" as main characters in the closing gestures of the novels in which they appear, turning the novel over to the experiences of the characters around them.

Many scenes involving Hugo have been rewritten to include other characters—in particular see two scenes from *Volume 1,* the first in which Henry and June fight at dinner; the second when Anaïs goes to the brothel at 32 rue Blondel. In the *Diary,* it is Joaquin who smooths out the battle between Henry and June; Henry later accompanies Anaïs to the brothel. But reading the "unexpurgated diary" *Henry and June* (the series is called "A Journal of Love") one discovers it was Hugo, on both occasions; and one is able to see the extent to which she "rewrites" scenes to fit with the integrity of the new figure—Joaquin and Henry, in these two cases, that she is using as her "character."

---

2. Nin, *Novel of the Future,* 63.

At any rate, according to Nin, for some purposes fiction serves better than the structure of a diary: "The old concept of chronological, orderly, symmetrical development of character died when it was discovered that the unconscious motivations are entirely at odds with fabricated conventions. Human beings do not grow in perfect symmetry."[3]

The Early Diary of Anaïs Nin, Volumes 1-4, chosen and excerpted by Rupert Pole, feel different: more lush, chattier, not as urbane. Though chronology has something to do with this. Her universe is fuller, of course—Hugo, references to whom were removed from the first publications by his own request, is back in it. But the volumes themselves include more—more doubt, more detail, more dailiness.

The "Journal of Love" series drawn from the "unexpurgated" diaries presents the most intensely personal writing and also (though perhaps these two are not unrelated?) the most poetry and lyrical description. They are also the most focused and targeted *as* selections or individual books, each dealing with a different and quite distinct phase in Nin's personal growth. In this they quite imitate the original diary series, which had unity within each title, at least for the first five volumes.

What remains to be seen (besides the final four years of Nin's life, two diaries she kept simultaneously called "The Book of Music" and "The Book of Pain" are not yet chronicled in print) is the diary *exactly as Nin wrote it.* Like with that other great American deep-sea diver, Emily Dickinson, there are levels upon levels of editorial interventions into Nin's actual text.

Some day, I hope we will see it.

Also, "The Book of Pain" and "The Book of Music." Cadence of lust. Syntax of sorrow.

---

3. Ibid., 84.

As for Nin's achievement in fiction, why shouldn't we want to—try to—alter the structures of fiction in order to see a life the way it is actually lived, rather than life according to that pattern, the accepted map of a story: rising action, climax, falling action, whatever. In the end, she became a Postmodern writer after all: "We know now that *we are composites in reality,* collages of our fathers and mothers, of what we read, of television influences, and films, of friends and associates, and we know we often play roles quite removed from our genuine selves."[4]

Carole Maso writes of her hope that the "weird, gorgeous vessel" of the form of the novel could include "musings, ideas, dreams, segues, shifts in key, athletic feats of imagination, leaps and swirls…small, nearly imperceptible progresses. The unarticulated arc of our lives."[5]

Maso's own novel *American Woman in the Chinese Hat* enacts an exploration of these abilities of a novel's structure. Throughout the book the narrator's language—her ability to communicate experience—to herself, to her lover, or to us—completely fails her. By the conclusion, like Duras' Lol Stein, she is bordering on the incomprehensible; Nin, for her part, says in her portrait of Sabina she "wanted to describe fragmentation without the disintegration that usually accompanies it."[6]

I trust in Maso's work the novel's possibility—that poetry feels so much guilt over—to be as hermetic and as blatant as it likes. To speak in codes or tongues, to tell the truth. But what's at stake for us emotionally in a piece of writing that tries to enact in its form the experience it seeks to reveal, the way Nin's novels do?

---

4. Ibid., 84.
5. Carole Maso, *Break Every Rule,* (Berkeley: Counterpoint, 2000), 24.
6. Nin, *Novel of the Future,* 163.

A book of poetry sometimes lacks chronology, geography, characters, consistency of narrator, of theme, of direction—it's pure remembrance, but a remembrance that can't be trusted…the details keep changing. It is the remembrance of apparently insignificant episodes, years in the past. As the reader progresses through such a book, she has to decide—if it's closure and formula she wants, she will slowly perhaps work hard to uncover the secret significance of the episode being described; but if she prefers to be carried along by the experience and the music of the language, then—

"Close the door and window upon the world for a moment, turn to the diary for all its musical notations, and begin another novel," Nin writes to herself at one point. The novel was a dream or an outline that the writer journeyed towards.[7]

So one has to ask: does the fracturing and fragmenting of experience into the pure music of language lead one anywhere? Is it all just surrealist or postmodern trickery?

The novel can have sculpture, a physical sense, a choreography, same as a poem. The novel and the poem both can sustain narrative or suppress it. But the poem applies pressure onto its subject: it's often driven by the formal requirements of line, page, and music. The novel, on the other hand, offers freedom—it is driven by content: subject and narrative and if by music, then the music of pure thought, rather than material language.

Novelists who work experimentally and/or musically— Carole Maso, Duras, Woolf, Fanny Howe, just for a few examples—are not constrained by the typical forms of fiction, e.g. setting, character, story arc, themes—but work intuitively with a poet's mind.

---

7. Nin, *Diary, Volume III*, 314.

These are books Djuna would not burn.

For me, Nin's novels approach a secret place where meaning happens. It is our temptation to leave the mysterious space around this place.

Perhaps this is the reason Sappho's poems, though shredded to bits, still resonate within us all as fragments.

Because real "meaning" is a river that flows *through* the mind and does not attempt to complete itself.

The writing of such books is one thing—the publishing of them is like the secret crossing of one's fingers.

It is tempting—it's the wish of the lyric poet, or perhaps of all poets—to leave language at the moment of the pitch into empty space, at the moment of the dare but not the dare's fulfillment. And ordinarily, one would suggest, as Carole Maso does, in her essay "Notes of a Lyric Artist Working in Prose," the novelist must continue past the moment of language's leap into the unknown, to learn "like sex, how to go past the intensity of the moment."[8]

But Nin doesn't. Or doesn't need to. She can take Djuna and Paul to the lip of the end of their relationship and leave them there. Or Lillian in the plane, on her way home, never arriving within the covers of the book. Or Djuna and Rango, walking along the quays after the storm, Djuna clear on the fact their relationship is over, but the "denouement" of the story never happens.

By the end of her fiction writing, Nin turns away from the grand structure, the intricate architecture toward the more improvisatory form of the collage. When Marguerite Young

---

8. Carole Maso, *Break Every Rule,* (Berkeley: Counterpoint, 2000), 23.

suggests each small episode of *Collages* could be its own book, Nin says, "I would lose the lightness of the rhythm... sometimes briefness, a semiabstraction can express mobility, a lyrical levitation which a full development might weigh down, even destroy."[9]

As in Woolf's *Between the Acts,* in all of Nin's novels the ending doesn't really get told, the ending is the dream—Djuna's reverie in music, or Renate eddying back to her beginning, because the structure of life and lived experience is the model for fiction.

"I always wanted to write a free book, a book as light and as humorous as the paintings of Paul Klee, Joan Miró, or the collages of Jean Varda," she wrote in *Novel of the Future.* "The ponderous, premeditated designs of novels always oppressed me."[10]

She sought new forms for fiction in other forms of art—whether dance, film, painting, or newer hybrid forms. She writes, "Jazz, collages, mobiles, animation in films, the combination of several arts have all indicated ways of renewal for the novel form."[11]

When I say Anaïs Nin made space in the novel, I mean space for both eros—the body and its sensual pleasures of experience—but also space for psyche, the mind and its intuitive qualities and ability to reach *sub*conscious levels of the self and of shared experience.

As I mentioned, Nin once said that, "Human beings do not grow in perfect symmetry." She goes on to clarify: "They oscillate, expand, contract, backtrack, arrest themselves, retrogress, mobilize, atrophy in part, proceed erratically,

---

9. Nin, *Novel of the Future*, 92.
10. Ibid., 126.
11. Ibid., 89.

according to experience and traumas...Some people are futuristic characters, some are cubistic, some are hard-edged, some geometric, some abstract, some impressionistic, some surrealistic..."

If Nin is absolutely contemporary in the 21st century, it is because by reconnecting with our deeper sources and urges we may finally learn how to live humanly. It's no less than the nature of identity and self and how these are constructed that are at stake in Nin's work.

That can be of no greater relevance than to our contemporary situation, lost in a world of hyperreality and the replacement of the concept of zero/infinity with the mere ever presence of endless information and "now"-ness that the electronic age both provides and demands.

In Nin's fiction we return to an interchange between sensuality and the mind that human existence is made of. "The novelist of the future," she suggests, "knows that a new psychological reality can be explored only under new conditions of atmospheric pressure, temperature and speed as well as in new terms of time and space, dimensions for which the old forms and conventions of the novel are completely inadequate."[12]

So in the new world, governed by instantaneous information, a turning of the individual physical erotic body into a commodity and the attendant dehumanizing political and social practices of late capitalism, Nin's work is more important than ever.

It can teach us the new human potential of our current knowledges.

---

12. Ibid., 173.

Bibliography

Alexander, Meena. *Poetics of Dislocation*. University of Michigan Press, 2009.

DuBow, Wendy, ed. *Conversations with Anaïs Nin*. University Press of Mississippi, 1994.

Duras, Marguerite. *The Ravishing of Lol Stein*. Translated by Richard Seaver. Pantheon, 1964.

Harryman, Carla. *Adorno's Noise*. Essay Press, 2010.

Hinz, Evelyn, ed. *A Woman Speaks: The Lectures, Seminars and Interviews of Anaïs Nin*. Swallow Press, 1979.

Hinz, Evelyn. *The Mirror and the Garden: Realism and Reality in the Writings of Anaïs Nin*. Harcourt Brace Jovanovich, 1973.

Jason, Philip K. *Anaïs Nin and Her Critics*. Camden House, 1993.

Maso, Carole. *Break Every Rule*. Counterpoint, 2000.

Nin, Anaïs. *Cities of the Interior*, with an introduction by Sharon Spencer. Ohio University Press, 1980.

Nin, Anaïs. *Collages*. Swallow Press, 1964.

Nin, Anaïs. *Henry and June: from the Unexpurgated Diary of Anaïs Nin*. HBJ, 1986.

Nin, Anaïs. *House of Incest*. Gemor Press, 1947.

Nin, Anaïs. *House of Incest*, with photomontages by Val Telberg. Swallow Press, 1958.

Nin, Anaïs. *In Favor of Sensitive Man and Other Essays*. HBJ, 1976.

Nin, Anaïs. *Solar Barque*, with illustrations by Peter Loomer. Edwards Brothers, 1958.

Nin, Anaïs. *The Diary of Anaïs Nin, Volume One: 1931-34*. HBJ, 1966.

Nin, Anaïs. *The Diary of Anaïs Nin, Volume Two: 1934-39*. HBJ, 1967.

Nin, Anaïs. *The Diary of Anaïs Nin, Volume Three: 1939-1944*. HBJ, 1969.

Nin, Anaïs. *The Diary of Anaïs Nin, Volume Four: 1944-1947*. HBJ, 1971.

Nin, Anaïs. *The Diary of Anaïs Nin, Volume Five: 1947-1955*. HBJ, 1974.

Nin, Anaïs. *The Diary of Anaïs Nin, Volume Six: 1955-1966*. HBJ, 1976.

Nin, Anaïs. *The Diary of Anaïs Nin, Volume Seven: 1966-1974*. HBJ, 1980.

Nin, Anaïs. *The Early Diary of Anaïs Nin, Volume Four: 1927-1931*, with a preface by Joaquin Nin-Culmell. HBJ, 1985.

Nin, Anaïs. *The Mystic of Sex: Uncollected Writings, 1931-1974*. Gunther Stuhlmann, ed. Capra Press, 1995.

Nin, Anaïs. *The Novel of the Future*. Ohio University Press, 1968.

Nin, Anaïs. *Under a Glass Bell*. Swallow Press, 1948.

Nin, Anaïs. *Waste of Timelessness*. Magic Circle Press, 1977.

Nin, Anaïs. *Winter of Artifice*. Swallow Press, 1946.

Nin, Anaïs. *The Winter of Artifice: A Facsimile of the Original 1939 Paris Edition*, with an introduction by Benjamin Franklin V. Sky Blue Press, 2007.

Richard-Allerdyce, Diana. *Anaïs Nin and the Remaking of the Self: Gender, Modernism and Narrative Identity*. Northern Illinois Press, 1998.

Sugisaki, Kazuko, "Staging the Dream: Japanese Noh Theater and the Fiction of Anaïs Nin" in *Anaïs Nin: An International Journal*. Gunther Stuhlmann, ed. Volume 6, 1988.

Acknowledgments

I am grateful to Fox Frazier-Foley, Steven Reigns, and Paul Herron for their feedback on this manuscript.

Furthermore, long overdue gratitude to Mary de la Torre, Chris Kelly, Deb DeGeorge, and Sloan Davis—when I first discovered Anaïs Nin, they were there along with me.

About the Author

Kazim Ali's books include poetry, fiction, essay, and hybrid form. He has translated books by Sohrab Sepehri, Ananda Devi and Marguerite Duras.

(dream chapter)

(Choreography for "Anaïs Nin: the I of the Storm,"
principal dancer Kazuo Ohno)

(dear deerspun spark dear emergent)

(when the first dancer emerges
from the group huddled upstage
it is as if he 'disappears' from their reality
they do not know where he has gone
nor does he)

(show not only gesture but full sensory and bodily awareness)

(of all bodies as speaking instruments)

(glue paper and feathers and shale to the body as wings)
(directly on the body so they will shed during the dance)

what role does light play here?
if the setting is external, how to schedule in concert with rain—

(flickering line of eight or ten dancers, but in the blue half-
light the audience

should not be able to distinguish individuals or even count the number of bodies)

(androgynous or genderqueer dancers should be used)
if the setting is internal how then to simulate not only sound but actual physical presence of rain—

(setting: a fishing village, factory town, abandoned church, frontier outpost)

in the night I

(first dancer moves with deliberation, cannot leave the earth. sinking action juxtaposed with leaps and jumps from younger. and then a shift to dramatic falls and rolls of the younger opposed to the gentle swaying upward draft of the first—)

(he is: a woman with long black and silver hair, long, unbound, swaying in explicitly sexual movements.

from the shoulder she slowly lifts the full arm, from the hip she moves her full leg.

no movement originates from the limbs only from deep within the torso.

you hear her the way you hear someone walking around in the apartment upstairs)

rain your crucial test of breathing

(lights against the fabric of the shirts
as the rain comes down harder, her white shirt becomes heavy, her hair curls and twists)

(there is a journey from the frenetic to the almost still

always the light dims as the sun slowly sets over the lip of the mountain

you are always so fearful to go out in the streets and look skyward)

> *and when the lights come up it is not yet*

why won't you ever whisper back to them ghosts in the dark and so lonely

dancer gestures desperately to the front row
waits for someone to ask her what she wants

(I thought I would die from the sight of such actual infinity,)

the dance continues, does not end, until someone responds to her, either with gesture or word—

(so close you could reach out and touch one another)

www.ingramcontent.com/pod-product-compliance
Lightning Source LLC
Chambersburg PA
CBHW040415100526
44588CB00022B/2834